ASPEN PUBLI

Friedman's
Practice Series

Evidence

Edited by

Professor Joel Wm. Friedman

Tulane University Law School
Jack M. Gordon Professor of Procedural Law & Jurisdiction

Wolters Kluwer

Law & Business

AUSTIN   BOSTON   CHICAGO   NEW YORK   THE NETHERLANDS

Aspen Publishers
Attn: Permissions Department
76 Ninth Avenue, 7th Floor
New York, NY 10011-5201

To contact Customer Care, e-mail customer.care@aspenpublishers.com, call 1-800-234-1660, fax 1-800-901-9075, or mail correspondence to:

Aspen Publishers
Attn: Order Department
PO Box 990
Frederick, MD 21705

Printed in the United States of America.

1 2 3 4 5 6 7 8 9 0

ISBN 978-0-7355-8624-6

About Wolters Kluwer Law & Business

Wolters Kluwer Law & Business is a leading provider of research information and workflow solutions in key specialty areas. The strengths of the individual brands of Aspen Publishers, CCH, Kluwer Law International and Loislaw are aligned within Wolters Kluwer Law & Business to provide comprehensive, in-depth solutions and expert-authored content for the legal, professional and education markets.

CCH was founded in 1913 and has served more than four generations of business professionals and their clients. The CCH products in the Wolters Kluwer Law & Business group are highly regarded electronic and print resources for legal, securities, antitrust and trade regulation, government contracting, banking, pension, payroll, employment and labor, and healthcare reimbursement and compliance professionals.

Aspen Publishers is a leading information provider for attorneys, business professionals and law students. Written by preeminent authorities, Aspen products offer analytical and practical information in a range of specialty practice areas from securities law and intellectual property to mergers and acquisitions and pension/benefits. Aspen's trusted legal education resources provide professors and students with high-quality, up-to-date and effective resources for successful instruction and study in all areas of the law.

Kluwer Law International supplies the global business community with comprehensive English-language international legal information. Legal practitioners, corporate counsel and business executives around the world rely on the Kluwer Law International journals, loose-leafs, books and electronic products for authoritative information in many areas of international legal practice.

Loislaw is a premier provider of digitized legal content to small law firm practitioners of various specializations. Loislaw provides attorneys with the ability to quickly and efficiently find the necessary legal information they need, when and where they need it, by facilitating access to primary law as well as state-specific law, records, forms and treatises.

Wolters Kluwer Law & Business, a unit of Wolters Kluwer, is headquartered in New York and Riverwoods, Illinois. Wolters Kluwer is a leading multinational publisher and information services company.

ABOUT THE EDITOR

Joel Wm. Friedman
Tulane Law School
Jack M. Gordon Professor of Procedural Law & Jurisdiction,
   Director of Technology
BS, 1972, Cornell University; JD, 1975, Yale University

Professor Joel Wm. Friedman, the Jack M. Gordon Professor of
Procedural Law & Jurisdiction at Tulane Law School, is the lead
author of two highly regarded casebooks — "The Law of Civil
Procedure: Cases and Materials" (published by Thomson/West)
and "The Law of Employment Discrimination" (published by
Foundation Press). His many law review articles have been
published in, among others, the Cornell, Texas, Iowa, Tulane,
Vanderbilt, and Washington & Lee Law Reviews.

Professor Friedman is an expert in computer-assisted legal instruction who has lectured throughout the
country on how law schools can integrate developing technologies into legal education. He is a past
recipient of the Felix Frankfurter Teaching Award and the Sumpter Marks Award for Scholarly
Achievement.

CONTENTS

Contents

Evidence Law
Essay Examination
QUESTIONS

EVIDENCE LAW ESSAY EXAM #1

QUESTION #1

John Jones is charged with burglary. During the presentation of its case-in-chief, the State offers the testimony of Officer Obee, who states that he and Officer Mulligan, on the day after the alleged offense, approached Jones at his home, explained that Jones was suspected of burglary, and fully advised Jones of his rights. Then, Officer Obee testifies that in response to a question as to Jones's whereabouts from between 8 and 10 o'clock the prior evening, Jones replied that he had spent that time seeing the movie "Rocky" at a downtown theater. The prosecutor then calls Officer Mulligan, who testifies that immediately after the burglary, he came upon the scene and was approached by a bystander who screamed, "I can't stand it! John Jones and I just robbed that store." During the presentation of his case, Defendant denies any involvement in the burglary. In its rebuttal case, the State offers certified copies of judgments rendered against Jones in two prior cases — a conviction for another burglary and a conviction for aggravated assault.

Discuss all objections that arguably could be raised with respect to each piece of evidence discussed in this question and then explain how and why the trial court would rule on such objections.

QUESTION #2

Acme Encyclopedia Company sells most of its books on a door-to-door basis. It will hire anyone who has access to a car as a sales representative. Dave Driver had been such a representative for seven months, when one evening, while driving to visit a prospective purchaser, Dave hit Polly Pedestrian. Polly sues Acme, seeking $150,000 in actual damages and $850,000 in punitive damages. Acme claims that it is not responsible for Dave's actions because he was an independent contractor who set his own hours, chose his own route, and contacted his own prospects. In her case-in-chief, plaintiff calls another Acme sales representative, who testifies that Acme, which also sells bookcases and popular magazines, has a policy of paying all its sales representatives on a straight commission basis and that the representatives are expected to pay all their own expenses, except that any sales person who has been with the company for more than three months receives 15 cents per mile for automobile expenses while on company business and is covered by a $200,000 liability insurance policy for any accidents that occur on company business. Plaintiff then calls a garage mechanic, who testifies that two days after the accident, he was asked to check out the steering and brake systems in the car and that his bill was paid by an Acme Company check. Finally, Polly calls Fred, a friend of Dave's who testifies that Dave always drove in excess of the speed limit and, that while a passenger in Dave's car on a prior occasion, he saw Dave run a red light and mangle a pedestrian, Sidney Springer, who had been carefully crossing the street.

During its cross-examination of Fred, Acme elicits testimony from Fred acknowledging that Fred had been a named cross-defendant in prior litigation between Springer and Dave.

Discuss all objections that arguably could be raised with respect to each piece of evidence discussed in this question and then explain how and why the trial court would rule on such objections.

QUESTION #3

Defendant Lorne Order is accused of murdering Herwitt Smintz, a wealthy merchant, on June 20, 2006. In its case-in-chief, the government calls Willie Wonka, an old friend of Lorne's, who testifies that while serving with Lorne in Iraq, he observed the glee with which Lorne went around killing people and that he, Willie, has concluded that Lorne is an extremely vicious and violent person. During her cross-examination of Willie, defense attorney Jane Victory asks Willie if he knew that Lorne had undergone psychiatric treatment after the war to attempt to deal with his aggressiveness.

After Lorne testifies to his complete and total innocence with regard to the instant charge, the prosecutor, in its rebuttal case, calls Saul Peter, another of Lorne's old friends. This witness testifies that once a week, he and Lorne went to the local supermarket and walked out with small cans of food without paying for them.

In the victim Smintz's probate proceeding, the legal heirs (those who would inherit if the will is declared invalid) claim that the deceased wrote his will in 2007 while subject to the undue influence of his nephew Harold, the sole named beneficiary under the will. (Undue influence is a ground for invalidating a will.) In support of their claim, the heirs offer the testimony of Bruce, the deceased's personal secretary, who states that at the time the will was being drafted, Smintz told Bruce that he was under extreme business pressure and therefore, to avoid spending any time on an unpleasant subject, simply was doing whatever his nephew suggested with respect to the terms of the will. To rebut this contention, Nephew Harold offers the testimony of the deceased's best friend, Irving, who states that while he and Smintz were playing a round of golf about one week before Smintz's death, Smintz said, "I gave a great deal of thought to who should be named in my will and finally concluded that since Harold is the only member of my family that I can trust, I decided to leave everything to him."

Discuss all objections that arguably could be raised with respect to each piece of evidence discussed in this case and then explain how and why the trial court would rule on such objections.

QUESTION #4

Bartender Hi Ball received a counterfeit $10 bill as a payment for a drink. Realizing it was counterfeit, he told the manager to call the police. When the police arrived, Hi pointed to Paul, the man who gave him the bill, and Paul was arrested. At

Paul's trial a year later, the arresting officer testifies that Paul is the man that Hi pointed out.

Discuss all objections that arguably could be raised with respect to each piece of evidence discussed in this case and then explain how and why the trial court would rule on such objections.

EVIDENCE LAW ESSAY EXAM #2

QUESTION #1

Plaintiff sued Jim's Department Store for personal injuries sustained when he fell from the store's only escalator. Defendant store's answer denied any negligence on its part and further contended that Plaintiff did not suffer any injury. Plaintiff testifies at trial that the escalator was running at an unreasonably fast speed, which caused him to fall as he tried to alight therefrom. On cross-examination, defense counsel asks Plaintiff if it is true that he is an alcoholic. Plaintiff's next witness, Will, testifies that he was on the escalator several days before Plaintiff's accident and that after almost falling off of it himself, he ran and told a store employee that the escalator was running dangerously fast.

During the presentation of its case, the defense offers certified copies of court records showing that Plaintiff previously had filed 20 unsuccessful personal injury suits during the past five years against various local stores, including two against Jim's. Defense counsel then offers a certified copy of a conviction rendered against Will for forgery (a statutory felony) in another state, eight years ago. The next witness for the defense, Al, an old friend of Plaintiff's, testifies that he thought that Plaintiff was a thoroughly dishonest person and a hypochondriac.

During his rebuttal case, Plaintiff offers the testimony of his wife, who states that she was with Plaintiff on the day of the accident and that when she returned to the store a week later, she overheard one mechanical engineer employee tell another: "Let's go outside for a beer. I'm exhausted from spending the last two hours slowing down the speed of that damned escalator."

Discuss both sides of all objections that could arguably be raised with regard to each piece of evidence discussed in this question and then explain how and why the trial court would rule on such objections.

QUESTION #2

Defendant is on trial for the murder of his business partner and asserts the defense of self-defense. It is established that the victim died from brain injuries caused by a skull fracture. The defendant, during his defense case, offers the testimony of Ray, the bookkeeper for the partnership, that on the day before the alleged murder Ray overheard a violent argument between the defendant and the deceased during which the deceased threatened to kill his partner if he found any evidence that the partner was stealing from the firm. The prosecutor, on rebuttal, calls defendant's ex-wife, who testifies that defendant beat her on several occasions when angered, once fracturing her skull.

Discuss both sides of all objections that could arguably be raised with regard to each piece of evidence discussed in this question and then explain how and why the trial court would rule on such objections.

QUESTION #3

Defendant is accused of murdering his wife and asserts a plea of guilty by reason of insanity. Several weeks after he was arrested and released on bond, defendant was ordered by the court to undergo a psychiatric examination, during which he told the psychiatrist that he did not know what he was doing at the time he began hacking his wife to pieces. At the pre-trial hearing to determine whether the defendant is competent to stand trial, the defense attorney introduces this statement through the testimony of the psychiatrist. At trial, the defendant offers the testimony of his best friend, Sal, who states that on the night before the alleged murder the defendant had asked for Sal's advice with respect to what the defendant should buy for his (the defendant's) wife for their upcoming tenth wedding anniversary. During rebuttal, the prosecutor calls witness Sam, who testifies that he has lived next door to defendant for 20 years and that he believes that Defendant has an extremely violent temper.

Discuss both sides of all objections that could arguably be raised with regard to each piece of evidence discussed in this question and then explain how and why the trial court would rule on such objections.

QUESTION #4

Plaintiff is injured when the car he was driving collided with a car owned by Otto Poor. As Dave, the driver of Otto's car, is lying face down on the ground with blood oozing out of the top of his head, he gasps to a passerby: "Tell the driver of the other car that I'm sorry I did not see the red light and that I'll pay all of his medical expenses if he promises not to sue me." In his personal injury suit against Otto, plaintiff calls the passerby to testify as to this statement. On cross-examination, the defendant's attorney gets the passerby to testify that he thought the plaintiff's car was traveling at about 65 mph at the moment before the accident.

Discuss both sides of all objections that could arguably be raised with regard to each piece of evidence discussed in this question and then explain how and why the trial court would rule on such objections.

QUESTION #5

Husband is suing wife for divorce on the grounds of adultery. Wife's answer denies this charge. At trial, husband calls Nurse Nancy, who testifies that on March 1, 2008, she overheard Doctor Dan (who had fled the country six months before the trial began) describe the details of his sexual involvement with Wife to someone over the telephone. Wife then offers the testimony of witness Greta, who states that she had a conversation with Dr. Dan on April 14, 2008, during which Dr. Dan complained about his inability to persuade Wife to be unfaithful to Husband.

Discuss both sides of all objections that could arguably be raised with regard to each piece of evidence discussed in this question and then explain how and why the trial court would rule on such objections.

EVIDENCE LAW ESSAY EXAM #3

QUESTION #1

Sonny Day sued to recover for injuries sustained to his right hand as a result of his use of an allegedly defective sunlamp at the Fat City Athletic Club. At the trial, Sonny produced evidence to the effect that his injuries were caused by the club's negligence in failing to provide adequate safety shields in its sunlamps, and that as a result of the overexposure, the skin on his right hand was so badly burned as to render that hand practically useless. In support of his claim of negligence, Sonny offered evidence that another club member had suffered third-degree burns on his face from using the same sunlamp one week before Sonny's confrontation with the subject lamp.

During the presentation of its defense case, the athletic club produced a representative of the sunlamp manufacturer, who testified that no such screening safeguards were available or necessary and that the over-exposure could only be attributed to Sonny's failure to walk away from the lamp after the expiration of the maximum exposure period recommended in the instructions located on the machine. The athletic club also produced witness Lucy Lips, who testified that on the night before Sonny over-exposed himself, a man named I. Pagliacci came running up to Lucy and told her that he, Pagliacci, had recently broken into the club and made off with the contents of the cash register, the special screening filter for the sunlamp, three dirty athletic supporters, and a spare clown's costume.

Disbelieving Sonny's claim regarding the loss of the use of his right hand, the athletic club had hired special investigator Shea Muss to keep Sonny under constant surveillance and document Sonny's movements with the use of a motion picture camera. Mr. Muss testified at trial that he had trailed Sonny for six days and that during that period, Muss saw and took motion pictures of Sonny painting the outside of his house and playing basketball with his kids. The movies were not offered into evidence.

In rebuttal, Sonny offered the testimony of a police officer that before Pagliacci's conversation with Lucy Lips, Pagliacci denied any connection with the athletic club heist when questioned by that officer. Finally, Sonny also offered evidence, in rebuttal, that subsequent to his injury, the athletic club put screening filters on its sunlamps that will hereinafter prevent the type of injury suffered by Sonny.

Discuss both sides of all objections that could arguably be raised with regard to each piece of evidence discussed in this question and then explain how and why the trial court would rule on such objections.

QUESTION #2

P sues D to rescind a contract for fraud and damages. At trial, D calls his secretary, Frederick Foulface, who was present at a pre-trial meeting between

D and P during which attempts were made to negotiate a settlement of this controversy. Fred offers to testify that P said at that meeting: "Well, maybe the representations weren't fraudulent — I'll dismiss the action for refund of the purchase price plus $50,000."

Discuss both sides of all objections that could be raised with regard to Freddie's testimony and then explain how and why the trial court would rule on such objections.

QUESTION #3

Karl Klutz sues Sarah Speedfreak for personal injuries allegedly sustained in an automobile accident. It is undisputed that Karl was carefully crossing Royal Street. Karl claims that Sarah negligently ran the stop sign at the corner of Royal and Dumaine. She denies this allegation. Karl alleges that the trauma caused by the accident, coupled with his history of mild cardiac problems, triggered a major cardiac arrest. In support of his claim of injury, Karl introduces a medical report written by Dr. Icon B. Bought, a cardiologist employed by Karl to treat Karl after the accident. In the report, Dr. Bought states that during the examination Karl told Bought: "I've had a history of heart trouble, but if Sarah had kept her eyes on the road, I never would have suffered the big one."

Is the report admissible? Discuss (1) all arguable objections and the responses thereto; and (2) how and why the court should rule on the objections.

QUESTION #4

Jim Brady, proprietor of a jewelry store, believes that his employee, Laurence Lightfingers, has been pilfering pieces of reasonably expensive jewelry from the store. Jim therefore discharges Laurence and brings a civil conversion action against him to recover the value of various pieces of jewelry missing from the store.

Jim's first witness, Stu L. Pigeon, testifies that he has known and lived next door to Laurence for the past ten years and that everyone in the neighborhood knows that Laurence has a habit of permanently borrowing nice pieces of jewelry without permission. Laurence testifies to the effect that he did not steal any jewelry from Jim's store. In rebuttal, Jim offers a certified copy of a grand larceny conviction rendered against Laurence only six months prior to the dates of the alleged thefts from Jim's establishment.

Discuss, in the manner required by the preceding questions, the admissibility of each piece of evidence.

QUESTION #5

Phil Purebreath sues American Tobacco Corp. in a wrongful death action to recover damages for his wife's death which, Phil claims, was caused by cancer produced by the company's cigarettes. Phil offers the testimony of Nurse Gimble that her former employer, a doctor and cancer specialist who is now deceased, gave Phil's wife cobalt treatment, a treatment traditionally used for cancer.

Discuss the admissibility of the evidence.

EVIDENCE LAW ESSAY EXAM #4

QUESTION #1

Emil Boudreaux, a resident of New Orleans, takes the St. Charles Avenue streetcar every day to his place of employment in the French Quarter. Emil is suing the City of New Orleans for personal injuries sustained when the streetcar made an abrupt stop at the intersection of St. Charles and Napoleon Avenues. His complaint alleges that the streetcar was going so fast that when it approached the intersection it had to stop suddenly when the traffic light changed from green to red, throwing him to the floor of the car. At the trial, the plaintiff, Emil, testified that "the streetcar was flying down St. Charles — much faster than normal." He then stated that immediately after the accident, the conductor, Bob, rushed to see if Emil was hurt and said that he was sorry for driving so quickly, but that he was behind schedule and that he usually did not drive so fast, and that he was sure that because the City was insured it would pay for any of Emil's medical bills. On cross-examination of Emil, the City's attorney asked whether Emil had filed any suit against the City of New Orleans during the past five years. After Emil denied filing any such suit, the City's attorney offered a digitally created copy of court records showing that Emil had filed 20 personal injury actions against the City of New Orleans during the past five years. Emil then offered the testimony of his friend, Tom, that he (Tom) had taken the streetcar a few weeks before Emil's accident and that he had complained to the conductor that he thought the conductor was driving much too fast. On cross-examination of Tom, the City's attorney asked Tom whether he ever had been arrested for gambling or prostitution or convicted of any vehicular misdemeanor offenses. The next witness called by the plaintiff, Jane, testified that she had known Tom for the past 20 years and that he was incapable of telling a lie. Finally, in its defense case-in-chief, the City offered the testimony of the Superintendent of Streetcar Conductors that one week after Emil's accident, the conductor, Bob, told the Superintendent that he had made the abrupt stop to avoid running into a jogger who had suddenly and unexpectedly darted out in front of the streetcar as it approached the intersection.

Discuss all arguments that could be raised in objection to and in support of the admission of each piece of evidence and state how and why the trial judge should rule on such objections.

QUESTION #2

Ray Lamb is indicted for possession with intent to sell 1,000 pounds of pure cocaine on March 16, 2008. Ray's defense is that he was delivering a package for a friend and was unaware of its contents. The prosecution's first witness, police Officer Friday, testified that on March 16, 2008, he and his partner, Officer Gannon, were on patrol when they responded to a call from headquarters over their radio directing them to 1300 Oak Street, where someone had reported hearing two gunshots. Upon their arrival, they found a man named Steve lying in a pool of blood. As Cleary bent down to see if the man was breathing, the man whispered, in a barely audible voice, "They got the wrong guy. I wasn't carrying the coke — Ray had it." The prosecutor then offered the following portion of a diary stipulated to have been written by Steve: "March 10, 2008 — Things are getting pretty tense — I don't know how I'm going to make the mortgage and car payments. Hopefully, everything will work out after Ray and I collect on a big coke sale set for the 16th." The prosecution's final witness is a paid informant, Louie, who testified that the defendant Ray had asked him to participate in the cocaine transaction and that he didn't dare refuse, particularly after having read several newspaper stories about organized crime that described Ray as "an enforcer for the mob." On cross-examination, Louie admits that he kept a diary but that he couldn't remember the entry for March 16, 2008. The defense attorney then offered that portion of the diary into evidence. The entry indicated that Louie was with Ray in another city on March 16, 2008, collecting on an overdue loan. On redirect, Louie testified that he had told the grand jury in this case that he and Ray had masterminded the cocaine sale on March 16, 2008. On direct examination, the defendant Ray proclaimed his innocence, denied involvement in the alleged cocaine transaction, and stated that over the past ten years he uniformly refused all solicitations to get involved in drug trafficking. On cross-examination, the prosecutor elicited an admission from Ray that he originally had entered a guilty plea after a series of negotiations with the prosecutor during which Ray confessed to the involvement in the sale and agreed to testify against his accomplices. The defendant's final witness, Mary, testified that she has lived across the street from the defendant for the past ten years and that he has a reputation for being a law-abiding, deeply religious family man. On cross-examination, Mary stated that she knew that Ray had been convicted of armed robbery and child abuse in 2003.

Discuss all arguments that could be raised in objection to and in support of the admission of each piece of evidence and state how and why the trial judge should rule on such objections.

> # EVIDENCE LAW ESSAY EXAM #5

> ## QUESTION #1

John P. Jamison, III is a second-term member of the U.S. House of Representatives from North Carolina charged with accepting bribes totaling $100,000 in exchange for his help in obtaining government contracts for private investors. Jamison is one of only four Congresspersons indicted as the result of a two-year-long investigation into racketeering and influence peddling conducted by the FBI. The prosecution's first witness was Rudy Claxton, an FBI agent who posed as Sven Boorking, a Norwegian oil developer seeking to do business with the U.S. government. Claxton testified that on February 3, 2008, in a meeting with Jamison and Jamison's attorney, the attorney stated Jamison would use his influence to get the federal government to accept Boorking's bid on an oil purchase contract in exchange for a $50,000 payoff. Claxton further testified that when he replied to the attorney that he (Claxton) was not able to pay more than $10,000, Jamison, according to Claxton's testimony, got extremely agitated and stated, "You've got to be kidding. I've never agreed to do this sort of thing before for less than $50,000." The government then called Senior Agent Ray Bresh, Claxton's supervisor at the FBI. Bresh testified that he believed Jamison was "the most corrupt person on the Hill," that he had seen Jamison angrily tear up the betting stubs at local horseracing tracks on three occasions during the past year, and that a reliable informant had told Bresh that Jamison was a frequent patron of a prostitution service run by that informant.

During the presentation of his defense case, Jamison took the stand and testified that he had never taken a bribe from anyone during his career as a public servant. In response to the prosecutor's question on cross-examination, Jamison stated that he always had been faithful to his wife during their 15-year-old marriage. Defense counsel then called Louis Bornwell, the senior Senator from North Carolina, who stated that he had known Jamison for 20 years and that Jamison was a thoroughly honorable man who never, to the Senator's knowledge, had taken a bribe from anyone.

After the conclusion of defendant's case, the trial judge allowed the government to call a few additional witnesses. One of them was Janice McDough, an old friend of Senator Bornwell's. McDough testified that one year before the trial she had received a letter from Bornwell lambasting a young Congressman, John Jamison, who, according to the letter, was a liar and a cheat. The prosecution also recalled Agent Claxton, who testified that he was instructed to go after Jamison by his boss at the FBI, because "my boss indicated that Jamison was reputed to be in desperate need of money to pay off heavy gambling debts and was susceptible to influence."

Discuss all objections that arguable could be raised with respect to each piece of evidence mentioned in this problem and then explain how and who the trial court would rule on those objections.

QUESTION #2

Lance Wilson was accused of murdering Jane Lane on April 1, 2008. The prosecution contended that Lance and Jane had been lovers and that Lance committed the murder after hearing that Jane had been having an affair with another man. One of the prosecution's key witnesses was Wilson's cousin, Bryan Flast. Flast testified that at 10:00 A.M. on April 2, 2008, a confused and exhausted Wilson came to Flast's home and told Flast that after overhearing Mark Pratt describe the affair Mark was having with Jane, Wilson returned to the home he shared with Jane and shot her. On cross-examination, defense counsel asked Flast to state where he was when defendant Wilson made this statement. Flast stated that the conversation took place in his home in Miami, Florida.

During the presentation of the defense case, counsel for the defendant called Margaret Phillips to the stand. Ms. Phillips testified that at 11:00 P.M. on April 1, 2008, Wilson telephoned her and said that he had just had a terrible argument with Jane and that although he had gone home with a gun and with the intent to kill Jane, he was unable to pull the trigger and left their home without touching her. The defense then called Bucky Wright, the hotel clerk at the Shady Inn Hotel in San Diego, California. Wright testified that he was working the front desk on the night of April 1, 2008. He further stated that according to the hotel register, Bryan P. Flast of Miami, Florida had registered as a guest at 10:00 P.M. on April 1, 2008. Wright also testified that while signing the register, Flast told him that Flast was planning to stay at the hotel for five days. To avoid putting the defendant on the stand, defense counsel sought to introduce a copy of a deposition in which Wilson stated that he did not kill Jane. Finally, the defense counsel sought to introduce a certified copy of a judgment rendered in favor of Wilson in a breach of contract action he had instituted against Flast.

Discuss all the objections that arguably could be raised with respect to each piece of evidence mentioned in this problem and then explain how and why the trial court would rule on those objections.

EVIDENCE LAW ESSAY EXAM #6

QUESTION #1

Jack Ryper, an organized crime figure, was charged with brutally murdering a police officer with a ceremonial sword that the officer had obtained during his service in the armed forces. The prosecution seeks to introduce six different photos of the decapitated victim lying in a pool of blood, each taken from a slightly different angle. It then offers the testimony of Sam, a neighbor of Ryper's, who states that everyone in the neighborhood knows that Ryper is a tough and violent guy. Sam then testifies that Ryper previously had been convicted of the theft of a ceremonial sword and various electronic devices from the decedent police officer's home. The prosecution then offers the testimony of Wanda, who states that she saw the defendant outside the police officer's home one hour before the murder occurred, standing in the rain next to his cherry red Lexus minivan. The defense subsequently calls Warren, who testifies that Wanda has a well-deserved reputation as a violent person and that he saw Wanda outside the police officer's home on the day in question and the sun was shining. On cross-examination of Warren, the prosecution gets Warren to admit that Wanda also has a well-deserved reputation as a truthful person. The prosecution offers the testimony of Louis that Louis saw the defendant lurking outside the police officer's home on the date in question. In response to a question on cross-examination, Louis admits that he had told a neighbor that he had been out of town on that same date in question.

The defendant claims that Ryper acted in self-defense. It offers the testimony of James Dunn, who testifies that he has known Ryper for 20 years and that Ryper is the type of guy "who always walks away from a fight." On cross-examination, the prosecution asks Dunn if he knows that Ryper had been convicted twice of tax evasion, to which he replies in the negative. The defendant then takes the stand and testifies that he had gone to the police officer's home to pay the longstanding monthly bribe and that the officer suddenly became violent and rushed at Ryper with a knife. During its cross-examination of the defendant, the prosecution offers evidence of the defendant's six-year-old conviction for armed robbery, a felony.

QUESTION #2

Henry Huggins brought a tort suit against Ellen, the owner of a supermarket, for $50,000 in damages after his luxury car fell into a huge hole in the supermarket's parking lot. Ellen alleged that the parking lot was owned by the city and thus she was not responsible for the plaintiff's injuries. Ellen was called as a witness by the plaintiff and on direct examination admitted that she unilaterally decided to repave the parking lot after suit was filed. The plaintiff Henry testified that during a pretrial conference, Ellen had told Henry that she probably should have paid closer attention to the condition of the parking lot and so she would give him $30,000 "to make this go away." The next witness, the supermarket's comptroller, Charles, answered in the affirmative to the plaintiff counsel's question as to whether or not the supermarket had liability insurance that covered the parking lot grounds. Witness Flora testified to seeing Huggins' car fall into a large ditch in the parking lot. On cross-examination, the supermarket's attorney offers evidence of Flora's five-year-old conviction for filing a knowingly false tax return and a two-year-old misdemeanor conviction for driving while intoxicated. Flora then admits that she lied in a previous lawsuit. The plaintiff then offers the testimony of Daniella, who states that her neighbor had told Daniella that the neighbor had been at the supermarket on the day of the accident and had been told by a supermarket cashier, "I cannot believe that another car fell into that darned pothole. When is the store going to patch that hole?" Another customer, Xavier, testifies that after viewing the accident, he went into the store to confront Ellen. Xavier testified that "I told Ellen that I knew that she had been aware of the hole in the parking lot for weeks and had done nothing to fix it and she said nothing in reply." Shirley Night was walking back to her car carrying a heavy bag of groceries when she observed Henry's car fall into the hole. At her advanced age, the burden of carrying that heavy bag proved to be too much for her and she suffered a heart attack, as a consequence of which she collapsed onto the ground, crushing her head on the concrete paving. Dr. Jones testified that he saw Shirley collapse and tried to revive her through mouth-to-mouth resuscitation. Ultimately, he was unsuccessful and Shirley passed away before the ambulance could arrive on the scene. Before she did, Jones testified, Shirley regained consciousness for a moment and said to Dr. Jones, "I saw that guy drive his car into the ditch, but he was driving with his eyes closed." Finally, after Yolanda, the supermarket's manager, testified that the store had never received any communications from the State Department of Consumer Affairs warning it of the problem caused by the hole in its parking lot, Glenda Brooks, the supermarket's assistant manager, admitted that she had seen Yolanda open a letter embossed with the State Department of Consumer Affairs logo on the front. The letter itself was not introduced into evidence.

Evidence Law
Essay Examination
ANSWERS

EVIDENCE LAW ESSAY EXAM #1

QUESTION #1

I. Obee's testimony re his statements to Jones

1. Definition of hearsay — Rule 801(c)   Obee's statements to Jones (1) that Jones was a burglary suspect and (2) advising Jones of his legal rights are both out-of-court statements. But neither of them is being offered to prove the truth of the matter asserted therein. Rather, they both constitute operative facts; i.e., each is being offered to prove that the statement was made to Jones and not that the contents of the statement are true. Consequently, neither meets the definition of hearsay because neither statement is being offered to prove the truth of the matter asserted. Rather, each is offered to establish the fact that it was made.

II. Obee's testimony of Jones' statement about seeing "Rocky"

1. Admission — Rule 801(d)(2)(A)   Obee is testifying as to an out-of-court statement that he heard from Jones, so that fits within the hearsay exception. And it is being offered to prove the truth of the matter asserted; i.e., that Jones had seen the movie "Rocky." But this is a statement by a party (the defendant) offered against the defendant. Consequently, it is an admission, which is deemed not to be hearsay under Rule 801(d)(2)(A). It does not matter whether or not the statement is against the declarant's interest. All statements made by a party offered against that party are deemed admissions and not hearsay.

III. Mulligan's testimony about bystander's statement

1. Excited utterance — Rule 803(2)   The officer is testifying as to an out-of-court statement (made by the bystander) offered to prove the truth of that statement (that John Jones robbed the store). It is therefore hearsay. But the exception in 803(2) for excited utterances allows admission of statements that (1) relate to a startling event (2) while the declarant (bystander) was under the stress of excitement caused by that event. The declarant does not need to be unavailable for this exception to apply. The facts indicate that the bystander screamed the statement concerning the alleged robbery and that it was made just after the alleged robbery. These facts suggests that the excited utterance exception would apply because the declarant appears to be under stress and the statement relates directly to the startling event — the robbery. The fact that the statement refers both to himself and the defendant does not affect the application of the excited utterance exception.

2. Declaration against interest — Rule 804(b)(3)   The officer is testifying as to an out-of-court statement offered to prove the truth of that statement. It is therefore hearsay. But under Rule 804(b)(3), if the declarant (bystander) is unavailable, the evidence would be admissible if the statement, at the time of its making, was contrary to the declarant's penal interest. The statement that he committed the robbery clearly is contrary to the declarant's penal interest. But the proponent of the evidence has the burden of persuasion to establish the declarant's unavailability. No evidence has been offered on unavailability, which means that the exception cannot be invoked and thus it is inadmissible hearsay. The party of the statement referring to John Jones as a participant in the robbery would not fall within the declaration against interest exception. This is viewed as a "collateral" statement, which the Supreme Court in *Williamson v. U.S.* (1994) held does not fall within the declaration against interest exception. Consequently, it remains hearsay and is inadmissible. Note that because the bystander's statement is not "testimonial" in the sense that it was not given while in custody, in response to police interrogation, nor in a context in which the bystander described that event while under the belief that he was supporting what he believed to be an investigatory or accusatory process, there is no Sixth Amendment Confrontation Clause issue relevant to its admissibility.

IV. Convictions offered against Jones

1. Character evidence of accused — Rule 404(a)(1) and Rule 405(a)   Under Rule 404(a)(1), the prosecution can offer evidence of the defendant's character for the circumstantial purpose of showing that he acted in conformity with that character and committed the charged crime ONLY after the defendant has opened the door by offering evidence of his good character. The defendant has not done that here and so the evidence of bad character is inadmissible. Moreover, under Rule 405(a), even if the defendant had opened the door, the prosecution could come forward with evidence only in the form of opinion or reputation. This is evidence of specific acts of the defendant and cannot be admitted on direct examination to show that he acted in conformity with the character trait associated with those past acts.

2. Impeachment of witness through extrinsic evidence of convictions — Rule 609   Because the defendant Jones testified as a witness, his character for truthfulness can be impeached by extrinsic evidence of prior convictions under the terms provided in Rule 609. The general rule that a witness cannot be impeached on the grounds of character for untruthfulness through the introduction of extrinsic evidence does not apply when that extrinsic evidence takes the form of either a felony conviction or of a conviction of a crime involving false statement or dishonesty. The two convictions here are for burglary and aggravated assault. Neither of these crimes fits within the Rule 609(a)(2) definition of a crime involving dishonesty or false statement. Consequently, if admissible, we must look to Rule 609(a)(1). Although these two crimes meet the Rule's requirement of being punishable by imprisonment in excess of one year, there is a special provision applicable when the witness whose credibility is being impeached is the criminal defendant, as in this case. Under these circumstances, the Rule provides that the trial judge can admit them only if the judge determines that the probative value of admitting this evidence outweighs its prejudicial effect to the accused. Because the accused in this case is accused of burglary, the prior burglary conviction might be deemed sufficiently prejudicial that it would be excluded under this balancing test. And the conviction for aggravated assault probably would be deemed to be of little probative value to establishing the truthfulness of the witness. Consequently, neither conviction should be admitted. Rule 609(b) also requires that the conviction not be more than ten years old (unless the judge determines that the probative value of an older conviction outweighs its prejudicial impact) and there is no evidence about this issue in the problem.

3. Authentication of physical evidence — Rule 902(4)   Physical evidence must be authenticated to be relevant and admissible, i.e., evidence must be offered to establish that it is what it purports to be. Under Rule 902(4), no extrinsic evidence of authenticity is necessary for a certified copy of public documents. Because the defense counsel offered certified copies of these convictions, the authentication requirement has been met.

4. Best evidence rule — Rule 1005   Because the defense counsel is offering the convictions to establish the contents of those writings, under Rule 1002, the best evidence rule is in play. But under Rule 1005, a certified copy of the conviction meets the requirements for offering an "original" of the writing whose contents are being established. Consequently, the best evidence rule requirement has been met here.

QUESTION #2

I. Testimony of Acme sales representative re: insurance coverage

1. Evidence of liability insurance — Rule 411   Under Rule 411, evidence that a person was insured against liability is not admissible if offered to establish that the person acted negligently or otherwise wrongfully. On the other hand, Rule 411 also states that evidence of having insurance is admissible to prove agency or control. Here, evidence that the driver employed by the defendant company was insured for liability for accidents occurring while driving on company business would not be admissible to establish the driver's negligence. But it would be admissible to establish an agency relationship between the driver and the defendant company which is relevant to the question of the company's vicarious liability for the actions of its employee while driving his own car on company business.

II. Testimony of garage mechanic

1. Definition of hearsay — Rule 801(c)   The mechanic testified that he was asked to check out the car. The request to check out the car was an out-of-court statement but it is not hearsay because it is an operative fact; i.e., the statement is being offered to prove that it was made. Thus its admissibility is not excluded under the hearsay rule.

2. Subsequent remedial measures — Rule 407   Under Rule 407, evidence that remedial measures were taken after injury was caused by some event is inadmissible to prove negligence on the part of the entity who took the subsequent remedial measures. This evidence is admissible, however, if offered to prove something else, such as control or feasibility of precautionary measures. Here, the evidence that the company paid for the mechanic's work would be inadmissible to prove the company's negligence but it would be admissible to establish the agency relationship between the company and the driver, a relevant fact because the case involves a claim of vicarious liability of the company for the acts of its employee sales representative.

3. Best evidence rule — Rule 1002   Here the mechanic testified as to the fact that he was paid by a check issued by the defendant company. By offering oral (secondary) testimony about the contents of a writing (the check) instead of offering the original writing itself, the proponent has raised an admissibility issue involving the best evidence rule. Under Rule 1004, secondary evidence of the contents of a writing can be admitted only upon a showing of the unavailability of the writing. Because the proponent of the secondary evidence has the burden of establishing unavailability, and that showing was not made, the oral recitation of the contents of the check would be inadmissible under the best evidence rule. However, if the fact that he was paid by check is not relevant, i.e., the fact that he was paid is important but not the manner in which he received payment, then the best evidence rule would not apply and the evidence would not be excluded under Rules 1002 and 1004.

III. Fred's testimony on direct examination

1. Character evidence — Rule 404   Under Rule 404, evidence of the character of a party (who was not also a witness) in a civil case that is offered for the circumstantial purpose of establishing that the individual acted consistently with that character trait is inadmissible, regardless of whether it is offered in the form of opinion, reputation, or specific prior acts. Thus, if the statement that Dave always speeded or previously ran a red light and hit a pedestrian (this is in the form of prior acts and not opinion or reputation) is treated as character evidence, it is inadmissible. However, under Rule 404(b), if evidence of prior acts is offered not to prove the actor's general character but some other issue, it would be admissible. Here, evidence of the employee's prior driving through a red light and mangling a pedestrian would be relevant to establishing the employer's notice of its employee's driving record and could be admitted for that purpose since this is a case alleging vicarious responsibility of the employer for its employee's conduct.

2. Habit evidence — Rule 406   Under Rule 406, evidence of a person's habit or routine practice, regardless of whether or not it is corroborated, is admissible to prove that the person acted consistently with that habit. To constitute habit, the conduct must be a routine response to a frequently occurring stimulus. If the trial judge determines that the statement that Dave "always drove in excess of the speed limit" refers to conduct that is sufficiently reflexive and repetitive, it would constitute habit evidence and be admissible to prove action in conformity with that habit in the instant case.

IV. Fred's testimony on cross-examination

1. Impeachment of witness for bias   The Federal Rules do not expressly address the subject of the manner in which a witness can be impeached for bias. Consequently, we must look to the common law for guidance. And though extrinsic evidence of specific conduct is admissible to show bias (though not to attack the character of the witness for truthfulness), here, the evidence came directly on cross-examination of the primary witness, Fred, and so the issue of extrinsic evidence is not present. This is proper impeachment–for–bias testimony.

QUESTION #3

I. Wonka's testimony on direct examination about Lorne's killings in Iraq

1. Character of accused — Rule 404(a)(1), Rule 405(a)   Under Rule 404(a)(1), the prosecution cannot offer evidence of the bad character of a criminal defendant for the circumstantial purpose of establishing that the accused acted consistently with that character in connection with the allegations in the instant case unless and until the defendant has opened the door by offering evidence of his good character. Because the defendant has not put his good character in issue, the prosecution cannot offer any evidence on this issue, regardless of whether it comes in the form of opinion, reputation, or specific acts. Moreover, under Rule 405(a), because the defendant's character is not directly in issue, even if the defendant had opened the door to circumstantial use of character evidence, such evidence would have to come in the form of opinion or reputation and not, as in this case, evidence of specific prior acts (Lorne's killing of individuals in Iraq).

II. Wonka's testimony on direct examination of Lorne's violent disposition

1. Character of accused — Rule 404(a)(1)   Under Rule 404(a)(1), the prosecution cannot offer evidence of the bad character of a criminal defendant for the circumstantial purpose of establishing that the accused acted consistently with that character in connection with the allegations in the instant case unless and until the defendant has opened the door by offering evidence of his good character. Because the defendant has not put his good character in issue, the prosecution cannot offer any evidence on this issue, regardless of whether it comes in the form of opinion, reputation, or specific acts. Thus, although this constitutes opinion testimony, a generally admissible form of character evidence, it is inadmissible because the defendant did not previously raise the issue of his good character.

III. Wonka's testimony on cross-examination

1. Character evidence — Rule 405(a)   Under Rule 405(a), once a witness offers reputation or opinion character evidence concerning the character of a non-witness, that character witness can be cross-examined on the foundation of that opinion through the introduction of evidence of prior acts of the person whose character the witness has testified about. In this case, the witness Wonka should not have been permitted to testify about Lorne's violent character because Lorne had not put the issue of his character into play. Consequently, if that testimony was stricken, so will this testimony be stricken. But if the trial judge mistakenly allowed the character testimony in the form of character witness Wonka's opinion to come in, Wonka can be asked on cross-examination whether he knew of prior acts of Lorne that were inconsistent with the character trait that he opined about. Because Wonka's testimony took the form of opinion testimony, asking whether he knew about this prior psychiatric treatment is relevant to impeaching the quality of the opinion testimony as it relates to Lorne's allegedly continuing violent character.

IV. Testimony of Peter

1. Character of accused — Rule 404(a)(1)   Under Rule 404(a)(1), the prosecution cannot offer evidence of the bad character of a criminal defendant for the circumstantial purpose of establishing that the accused acted consistently with that character in connection with the allegations in the instant case unless and until the defendant has opened the door by offering evidence of his good character. Because the defendant has not put his good character in issue, the prosecution cannot offer any evidence on this issue, regardless of whether it comes in the form of opinion, reputation, or specific acts. Moreover, under Rule 405(a), because the defendant's character is not directly in issue, even if the defendant had opened the door to circumstantial use of character evidence, such evidence would have to come in the form of opinion or reputation and not, as in this case, evidence of specific prior acts.

2. Habit testimony — Rule 406   Although evidence of a person's habit can be introduced to show that the person acted consistently with that habit, habit requires a regularized response to a frequently repetitive stimulus. The act of going to supermarkets and stealing small cans of food does not satisfy this standard, and so this testimony would not be admissible as habit evidence.

3. Witness impeachment — Rule 608   The defendant has testified and so he can be impeached by offering evidence of his character for untruthfulness. Under Rule 608, however, this evidence has to come in the form of opinion or reputation. Here, this is evidence of specific acts, and so therefore is inadmissible. Moreover, Rule 608(b) expressly precludes offering extrinsic evidence of specific instances of the witness's conduct not amounting to a conviction for the purpose of attacking his character for truthfulness except on cross-examination of that witness or of a character witness attesting to the original witness's character. This evidence was introduced on direct examination of a character witness and therefore is inadmissible for this reason as well.

V. Testimony of Bruce

1. Definition of hearsay — Rule 801(c)   Bruce is relating the out-of-court statement by Smitz to prove the truth of the matter asserted within that statement. It is hearsay, but it is also direct evidence of the declarant Smitz's then-existing state of mind (which is a relevant issue in the case), and therefore is subject to the Rule 803(3) exception and admissible to prove the truth of the matter asserted, i.e., that he was under stress and was unwilling to disagree with his nephew. Because this fits within the Rule 803(3) exception, there is no requirement that the declarant be shown to be unavailable.

VI. Testimony of Irving

1. Definition of hearsay — Rule 801(c)   Irving is relating the out-of-court statement by Smitz to prove the truth of the matter asserted, i.e., his decision to leave everything to his nephew. This does not fit within the present state of mind exception of Rule 803(3) because the declarant is relaying his past state of mind, i.e., a decision he already reached. Thus, it is inadmissible hearsay.

2. Impeachment of hearsay declarant — Rule 806   Under Rule 806, the credibility of a hearsay declarant can be attacked as if the declarant had been a witness. The rule expressly states that an inconsistent statement made at any time, i.e., before or after the admitted hearsay declaration, is not subject to the requirement that the hearsay declarant be given an opportunity to explain or deny the inconsistent statement. Here, the hearsay declarant is Smintz. His initial hearsay statement was admitted under Rule 803(3) and his subsequent inconsistent statement can be admitted to impeach his credibility under Rule 806. The fact that this is not a prior inconsistent statement does not matter; Rule 806 covers all inconsistent statements made at any time by a hearsay declarant.

QUESTION #4

I. Testimony of arresting officer

1. Definition of hearsay statement — Rule 801(a)   The police officer is repeating what he saw Hi do. But Hi's conduct in pointing out Paul was assertive conduct, i.e., it was conduct that was intended as an assertion. Consequently, it falls within the definition of a "statement" for hearsay purposes. Thus, the police officer is repeating an out-of-court statement that is offered to prove the truth of the matter asserted and so this is hearsay and inadmissible. It does not fit under any exception. It is not an excited utterance, because there has been no showing that Hi was under stress when he made the statement. It is not a present sense impression, because Hi was not describing something that he had just seen. Finally, it is not a prior statement of identification by a witness within the meaning of Rule 801(d)(1)(C) because Hi was not a witness at this trial.

EVIDENCE LAW ESSAY EXAM #2

QUESTION #1

I. Plaintiff's testimony on direct examination

1. Opinion testimony — Rule 701   The plaintiff's statement that the escalator was running "at an unreasonably fast speed" is a statement of opinion, and so is subject to the requirements of Rule 701. Although it is based on his personal knowledge of observing the escalator and may be rationally connected to that knowledge, the question is whether or not it is useful to the jury. This is a close call. It most likely would be viewed as useful to the jury because the plaintiff, and not they, could see and feel the impact of the speed of the escalator. This does not displace the function of the jury to determine whether or not this constitutes negligence on the part of the company. Therefore, it is admissible. The opinion, on the other hand, certainly does not meet the expert testimony requirement of Rule 702 because, among other things, the plaintiff was not qualified as an expert on the speed of escalators. However, it easily could be argued that judging whether or not an escalator was running at an unreasonably high speed is probably not the type of opinion that would be required to be made only by an expert. It is not based on scientific, technical, or other specialized knowledge, as required by Rule 701. This is a close call but probably admissible as a lay opinion.

II. Plaintiff's testimony on cross-examination

1. Character evidence — Rule 404   Evidence of the character of a non-witness in a civil case is not admissible for the circumstantial purpose of establishing that the person acted in conformity with that character trait, regardless of whether it takes the form of opinion, reputation, or past acts testimony. Consequently, this evidence is inadmissible to establish that the plaintiff acted consistently with the character traits associated with being an alcoholic and that this was the cause of his injury. However, the plaintiff was a witness. See the next answer.

2. Witness impeachment — Rule 608   The plaintiff testified at trial and so he is subject to impeachment as a witness. But under Rule 608(a), his character for truthfulness can be attacked only by evidence in the form of reputation or opinion. Here, the plaintiff was asked if he was an alcoholic. Under Rule 608(b), prior acts of a witness can be inquired into on cross-examination as long as they are probative of the witness's character for truthfulness or untruthfulness. Because the witness was asked directly about this, this is not a problem of offering extrinsic evidence of the witness's prior acts. But asking the plaintiff/witness whether he is an alcoholic goes to past acts that do not relate to truthfulness or untruthfulness. Consequently, this question is improper and the answer is inadmissible.

III. Testimony of Will

1. Definition of hearsay — Rule 801(c)
Excited utterance — Rule 803(2)
Present sense impression — Rule 803(1)   The witness Will is relaying the contents of his out-of-court statement. It would be hearsay if it is being offered to prove the truth of the matter asserted therein. Thus, it is inadmissible to prove that the escalators were running dangerously fast unless this statement fits within an exception. For the excited utterance exception of Rule 803(2) to fit, the declarant would have to be under the stress of an exciting event and be describing that startling event. Will did run and tell the manager about the escalators immediately after nearly falling off of it and so this exception could apply. Because this is a Rule 803 exception, the declarant does not have to be shown to be unavailable. Alternatively, the statement could be considered a present sense impression under Rule 803(1), because it describes what the declarant observed immediately after observing it. Because this is a Rule 803 exception, the declarant does not have to be shown to be unavailable.

Alternatively, the statement could be admitted not for the truth of the matter asserted, but merely to establish that the employer heard it — i.e., that it was on notice about the situation of its escalators, a relevant issue in this case. In this situation, the statement would not be hearsay and would be admitted.

2. Opinion testimony — Rule 801   Will's statement that the escalator was running "dangerously fast" is a statement of opinion that does meet the requirements of Rule 801. It is based on his personal knowledge of observing the escalator and may be rationally connected to that knowledge. And it is useful to the jury because he, and not they, could see and feel the impact of the speed of the escalator. This does not displace the function of the jury to determine whether or not this constitutes negligence on the part of the company. Therefore, it is admissible. The opinion, on the other hand, certainly does not meet the expert testimony requirement of Rule 702 because, among other things, the plaintiff was not qualified as an expert on the speed of escalators. However, it easily could be argued that whether or not an escalator was running at an unreasonably high speed is probably not the type of opinion that would be required to be made only by an expert. It is not based on scientific, technical or other specialized knowledge as required by Rule 701. This is a close call, but probably admissible as a lay opinion.

IV. Court records of plaintiff's prior suits

1. Public records exception to hearsay — Rule 803(8)   This is an out-of-court statement offered to prove its truth but clearly fits within the public records exception to hearsay in Rule 803(8).

2. Best evidence rule — Rule 1005   Under Rule 1005, the certified copies of this public record meet the requirements of the best evidence rule.

3. Character evidence — Rule 404   Under Rule 404, evidence of the character of a non-witness in a civil case is not admissible for the circumstantial purpose of establishing that the person acted in conformity with that character trait, regardless of whether it takes the form of opinion, reputation, or past acts testimony. So the evidence of the plaintiff's prior filing of lawsuits to establish his character of being

unsuccessfully litigiousness is not admissible to prove that he is filing a nonmeritor-
ious suit on this occasion.

4. Habit evidence — Rule 406   Under Rule 406, evidence of a person's habit
or routine practice, regardless of whether or not it is corroborated, is admissible to
prove that the person acted consistently with that habit. To constitute habit, the
conduct must be a routine response to a frequently occurring stimulus. A history of
filing unsuccessful lawsuits does not meet this definition of habit and therefore is
inadmissible under this theory.

5. Witness impeachment for bias   Because the Federal Rules do not expressly
address the subject of the manner in which a witness can be impeached for bias, we
must look to the common law for guidance. Bias can be established by extrinsic
evidence of prior acts by the witness. Here, the bias of the plaintiff/witness is
attempted to be shown through evidence that he previously and unsuccessfully
sued the same store that is the defendant in this case. That information is admissible
for the limited purpose of establishing his bias against the defendant and therefore
impeaching his credibility as a witness, but it is not admissible to establish the lack of
merit of the instant case.

6. Authentication — Rule 902(4)   Physical evidence must be authenticated to
be relevant and admissible, i.e., evidence must be offered to establish that it is what it
purports to be. Under Rule 902(4), no extrinsic evidence of authenticity is necessary
for a certified copy of public documents. Because the defense counsel offered certified copies of these court records, the authentication requirement has been met.

7. Best evidence rule — Rule 1005   Because the defense counsel is offering the
convictions to establish the contents of those writings, the best evidence rule,
Rule 1002, is in play. But under Rule 1005, a certified copy of the court records
meets the requirements for offering an "original" of the writing whose contents are
being established. Consequently, the best evidence rule requirement has been met here.

V. Forgery conviction

1. Impeachment of witness through extrinsic evidence — Rule 609(a)(2)
Although Rule 608(b) precludes the use of extrinsic evidence to impeach the
character for truthfulness of a witness, Rule 609(a)(2) creates an exception when
the conviction is for a crime involving false statement. Here, the conviction is for
perjury and so is admissible under Rule 609(a)(2), but only to impeach the witness
Will's credibility as a witness.

2. Authentication — Rule 902(4)   Physical evidence must be authenticated to
be relevant and admissible, i.e., evidence must be offered to establish that it is what it
purports to be. Under Rule 902(4), no extrinsic evidence of authenticity is necessary
for a certified copy of public documents. Because the defense counsel offered a
certified copy of the conviction, the authentication requirement has been met.

VI. Testimony of Al

1. Character evidence — Rule 404   Evidence of the character of a non–witness
in a civil case is not admissible for the circumstantial purpose of establishing that the
person acted in conformity with that character trait, regardless of whether it takes the

form of opinion, reputation, or past acts testimony. Thus, opinion testimony that the plaintiff is a liar and hypochondriac is inadmissible to prove that he acted in conformity with those traits in this case. But the plaintiff also was a witness, so see the next answer.

2. Impeachment of witness — Rule 608 Because the plaintiff testified, he is subject to impeachment by evidence of reputation or opinion going to his untruthfulness. Because Al is offering opinion testimony going to the plaintiff's untruthful character, this is admissible under Rule 608(a). But the opinion that the plaintiff is a hypochondriac does not go to truthfulness, and so is not admissible under Rule 6087(a).

3. Opinion testimony — Rules 701 and 702 Al has given his opinion that the plaintiff is a hypochondriac. This would appear to be a medical judgment requiring specialized knowledge and therefore not a permissible lay opinion under Rule 701. Because Al has not been qualified as an expert, the testimony cannot be admitted as expert testimony under Rule 702.

VII. Testimony of plaintiff's wife

1. Admission — Rule 801(d)(2)(D) The wife is repeating what she heard an employee say out of court and it is being offered to prove the truth of the matter asserted, i.e., that they just fixed the escalator. But it is also a statement by an agent of the defendant concerning a matter (maintenance of the escalator) within the scope of that agent's employment that is offered against the employer defendant. Thus, under Rule 801(d)(2)(D), it constitutes an admission. Consequently, it is not hearsay and is not excluded under Rule 802.

2. Subsequent remedial measure — Rule 407 Under Rule 407, evidence that remedial measures were taken after injury was caused by some event is inadmissible to prove negligence on the part of the entity who took the subsequent remedial measures. This evidence is admissible, however, if offered to prove something else, such as control or feasibility of precautionary measures. Here, the statement by the employee is offered to prove that the remedial measures were taken for the purpose of establishing the company's negligence. Consequently, it is inadmissible. There is no indication that the store had suggested the infeasibility of precautionary measures and so it cannot be admitted to rebut such a charge.

QUESTION #2

I. Testimony of Ray

1. Definition of hearsay — Rule 801(c) Ray is repeating what the deceased said out of court. However, the declaration is being offered not to prove the truth of the matter asserted (that the deceased truly intended to kill the defendant), but the state of mind of the defendant, the person who heard that statement. This is relevant to the defendant's self-defense claim because it goes to the defendant's state of mind concerning his fear of the deceased. This is a non-hearsay use of the statement and it is admissible to show the listener's state of mind.

2. State of mind — Rule 803(3)   Even if the declarant's out-of-court statement was offered to prove the truth of that statement, this statement directly reflects the declarant's present state of mind within the meaning of the hearsay exception codified at Rule 803(3). Moreover, under the *Hillman* doctrine, the statement is admissible to establish that the declarant attempted to follow through on this intended course of action.

3. Statement against interest — Rule 804(b)(3)   The deceased's out-of-court statement also was against his penal interest at the time it was made. Because the declarant is dead, he is unavailable, and so the statement is admissible as a declaration against penal interest under Rule 804(b)(3).

II. Testimony of Ex-wife

1. Character evidence of accused — Rule 404(a)(1)
Form of character evidence — Rule 405
Discretionary exclusion — Rule 403   Under Rule 404(a)(1), the prosecution can offer evidence of the accused's character for the circumstantial purpose of showing that the accused acted in conformity with that character trait but only after the defendant has opened the door by offering evidence of his good character and only through the introduction of opinion or reputation testimony. Because the defendant has not yet opened the door by offering evidence of his good character, the prosecution cannot offer evidence, in any form, of his bad character. Moreover, even if the defendant had opened the door, the prosecution would be limited under Rule 405(a) to offering, on direct examination, opinion or reputation testimony and this is evidence of prior bad acts.

However, under Rule 404(b), if evidence of the defendant's prior bad acts is offered not to show his character and action in conformity therewith, but some other matter, such as modus operandi or common plan, it would be admissible for that limited purpose. Because the deceased was killed by a skull fracture and the evidence the wife offers is of the defendant fracturing her skull, it might be admissible on this ground. But the similar nature of the alleged crimes might also convince the judge that the prejudicial impact would outweigh substantially any probative value, and so the evidence might also be excluded under Rule 403.

QUESTION #3

I. Testimony of psychiatrist

1. Medical diagnosis statements — Rule 803(4)   The psychiatrist testified as to what he heard the defendant say out of court and it is being offered to prove the truth of the matter asserted (that the defendant did not know what he was doing at the time of the murder). So, it is hearsay. But if it was a statement made for the purpose of aiding the doctor in providing diagnosis or treatment, it is admissible as an exception to the hearsay rule under Rule 803(4). Because the defendant was not meeting with the psychiatrist for treatment, but only to give the psychiatrist a basis for determining his competency, this exception would not apply.

2. State of mind — Rule 803(3)   This out-of-court statement does not fall within the state of mind exception to the hearsay rule because it does not reflect the declarant's present state of mind. It is memory as to his prior state of mind when he killed his wife. Therefore, this hearsay exception does not apply.

3. Physician-patient privilege   Although there is no physician–patient privilege recognized at common law, nearly all (but not all) states have enacted some variation of this privilege. In those states with a statutory privilege, the privilege typically extends to (1) confidential statements that are (2) made to a physician (3) for the purpose of obtaining treatment. This statement was made in the course of a doctor-patient relationship, but it was not made for the purpose of diagnosis leading to treatment. Consequently, it is not privileged.

4. Admission — Rule 801(d)(2)(A)   This is a statement by a party. But it is being offered by that party, the defendant. Thus, it is not an admission, because admissions are only statements by a party used against that party. So, it constitutes hearsay and is not saved by the exceptions discussed above.

II. Testimony of Sal

1. Definition of hearsay — Rule 801(c)   Sal testifies as to the defendant's out-of-court statement. But this statement is not being offered to prove the truth of the matter asserted therein, i.e., that the defendant wanted to know from Sal what to buy for his wife. Instead, it is being offered as circumstantial proof of the defendant's state of mind concerning his wife, i.e., that he loved his wife and did not intend to kill her. Consequently, it is not hearsay and is admissible for that purpose, i.e., to show his tender feelings towards his wife, which is relevant to the charge of murder.

III. Testimony of Sam

1. Character evidence of accused — Rule 404(a)(1)   Under Rule 404(a)(1), the prosecution can offer evidence of the accused's character for the circumstantial purpose of showing that the accused acted in conformity with that character trait, but only after the defendant has opened the door by offering evidence of his good character and only through the introduction of opinion or reputation testimony. Because the defendant has not yet opened the door by offering evidence of his good character, the prosecution cannot offer evidence, even this otherwise admissible form of opinion testimony, of his bad character.

2. Impeaching credibility of hearsay declarant — Rule 806   Although the defendant did not testify, he did make out-of-court statements to the psychiatrist and to Sal. The statement to the doctor was inadmissible hearsay that was not subject to the physician-patient privilege. (The statement to Sal, on the other hand, was not hearsay because it admitted for the limited purpose of showing the declarant's state of mind.) If a hearsay statement has been admitted into evidence, the hearsay declarant's credibility can be attacked under Rule 806 by any evidence that would be admissible to challenge credibility if that individual had testified as a witness. The evidence offered here is opinion testimony, but opinion as to the declarant's violent temper. This is not pertinent to challenge his credibility as a witness/hearsay declarant and therefore is inadmissible for the purpose of impeaching his credibility as a hearsay declarant.

QUESTION #4

I. Testimony of passerby on direct examination

1. Dying declaration   The passerby testifies to the out-of-court statement by Dave and it is being offered to prove the truth of the matter asserted (that Dave ran through the red light and will pay all medical expenses). So, it is hearsay. Part of it may fit, however, within the dying declaration exception of Rule 804(b)(2). This statement was made under belief of impending death, this is a civil action, and part of the statement concerns the cause of the declarant's impending death. But under Rule 804(b)(2), the declarant also must be unavailable, and this must be established by the party offering the testimony. Because there is no evidence that the declarant Dave is now dead or otherwise unavailable, the statement does not fall within the exception. If he is dead, however, than the portion of the statement concerning the red light would be admissible. But the statement referring to his offer to pay medical expenses does not concern the cause of his death, and so it does not fall within this exception even if Dave is unavailable.

2. Excited utterance — Rule 803(2)   This exception would apply only if Dave was under the stress of excitement caused by the accident when he made that statement concerning the exciting event. Although Dave is nearly dead, he does not appear to be excited; stressed, yes, but excited, no. The rule requires the declarant to be under the stress of excitement. Thus, this exception would not apply.

3. Declaration against interest — Rule 804(b)(3)   The statement that he ran the red light is against Dave's pecuniary interest when made. Even if he did not expect to survive, the statement could be contrary to the pecuniary interest of his estate. The remaining question, then, would be whether or not he is available. If the proponent of the testimony cannot establish that Dave is unavailable, this exception will not apply.

4. Payment of medical expenses — Rule 409   Under Rule 409, evidence of offering to pay medical expenses is not admissible to prove liability for the injury. So, the statement offering to pay the victim's medical expenses would be inadmissible under Rule 409.

II. Testimony of passerby on cross-examination

1. Opinion testimony   Calculating the speed of a car is deemed to be permissible lay opinion testimony under Rule 701. It aids the jury because they did not see the car. It is based on the witness's first-hand knowledge and rationally related to what he saw, and does not rely on specialized knowledge. So, it is admissible lay opinion testimony.

QUESTION #5

I. Testimony of nurse Nancy

1. Declaration against interest — Rule 804(b)(3)
  Unavailability of declarant — Rule 804(a)(5)   This is a hearsay statement because the witness Nancy is reporting what she heard the declarant Doctor Dan say out of court and the statement is offered to prove the truth of its contents, i.e., that

Dan was having an affair with the wife. But the statement is against the declarant Doctor's penal and pecuniary interests, as it could subject him to an adultery charge or civil liability for alienation of affection. So, the question that remains is whether the declarant is unavailable. The proponent of this testimony must establish that the declarant is unavailable as required by Rule 804(b)(3). Dan left the country before trial and therefore is unavailable within the definition of that term codified at Rule 804(a)(5), because he cannot be subpoenaed by the proponent of the Nurse's testimony or compelled to appear by other reasonable means. Consequently, the testimony is admissible as it falls within the Rule 804(b)(3) exception.

II. Testimony of Greta

1. Impeachment of hearsay declarant — Rule 806   Because the doctor's hearsay statement is admissible under Rule 804(b)(3), his credibility can be attacked under Rule 806. His credibility can be attacked in all of the ways that a witness's testimony can be attacked. Here, the wife is attempting to impeach the hearsay declarant's credibility by offering evidence of a statement inconsistent with his hearsay statement that he was having a sexual relationship with the wife. The fact that this inconsistent statement was made after, rather than prior to, the hearsay declaration is irrelevant under Rule 806. A hearsay declarant can be impeached by any inconsistent statement, regardless of whether it was made before or after the hearsay declaration. Moreover, the hearsay declarant need not be offered an opportunity to deny or explain the inconsistent statement, and so the fact that the hearsay declarant Doctor Dan is unavailable does not prevent this statement from being admitted to impeach his credibility. However, it is not admissible to establish the truth of the matter asserted in the Doctor's out-of-court declaration, i.e., that the wife refused to engage in a sexual relationship with him.

2. Definition of hearsay — Rule 801(c)   Greta's retelling of the doctor's out-of-court statement is inadmissible hearsay if it is offered to prove the truth of the matter asserted therein, i.e., that the wife refused to have sexual relations with Doctor Dan. Although that evidence would be relevant to her denial of adultery, it is inadmissible hearsay that does not fall within any exception as it is not a declaration against interest, a dying declaration, an excited utterance, etc. The hearsay declarant is Doctor Dan and not the wife, so the statement is not an admission.

EVIDENCE LAW ESSAY EXAM #3

QUESTION #1

I. Prior burning

1. Relevance — Rule 401   The evidence that another member had suffered burns to his face would meet the relevance test of Rule 401 as long as the proponent of the evidence also demonstrated that the circumstances under which he was burned were nearly identical to those affecting the plaintiff. If that is done, then the evidence can be admitted for the purpose of proving causation. On the other hand, if the evidence is offered solely for the purpose of proving that the club was on notice that there was a problem with its machinery, then the circumstances under which both individuals were burned do not have to be that similar.

II. Testimony of manufacturer's representative

1. Opinion testimony — Rule 702   The statement by the representative concerning nonfeasibility of preventive measures would appear to be expert testimony because it requires specialized knowledge. Under Rule 702, if the witness is qualified, he can offer expert testimony and it does not have to be based on his first-hand knowledge. But his statement concerning the cause of Sonny's injury may be a different story. It would appear to require specialized medical knowledge rather than specialized knowledge about this type of machinery. If so, then the testimony would be inadmissible as not within the area of the expert's specialization.

III. Testimony of Lucy lips

1. Definition of hearsay — Rule 801(c)   Lucy is repeating the out-of-court statement made by Pagliacci for the purpose of proving the truth of the matter asserted therein. Thus, this statement is hearsay. The question is whether it falls under any exception.

2. Statement against interest — Rule 804(b)(3)   Pagliacci's statement that he stole money from the register, a filter, a costume, and athletic supporters is against his penal and pecuniary interest because it could subject him to criminal prosecution for theft and civil liability for conversion of property. Therefore, it fits within the Rule 804(b)(3) exception if it is established that he is unavailable within the meaning of Rule 804(a). The proponent of the evidence has the burden of establishing unavailability, and there is no evidence here that Pagliacci is unavailable. Consequently, if he is not shown to be unavailable, the exception cannot apply and the evidence will be excluded because it is hearsay.

3. Excited utterance — Rule 803(2)   The hearsay statement by Pagliacci could be considered an excited utterance under Rule 803(2) if it was made while Pagliacci was under the stress of excitement of a startling event and related to that event. The facts indicate that Pagliacci came running up to Lucy and told her that he had "recently" broken into the club. Depending upon how recently the break-in had occurred and his mental state, if the proponent of the evidence can establish that Pagliacci was still feeling the exciting effects of the robbery, the evidence would be allowed in as an exception to the hearsay rule. Because this is an exception under Rule 803, the hearsay declarant, Pagliacci, would not have to be unavailable for the exception to apply.

4. Relevance — Rule 401   Pagliacci's statement concerning his theft of any of all of the items other than the screening filter is irrelevant because this is a tort action brought by Sonny against the club. There is no indication as to why evidence of Pagliacci's thievery from the club of items other than the screening filter is probative of a relevant issue in that case. But his statement that he stole a screening filter is relevant to the question of whether screening safeguards were available, which is part of the athletic club's defense.

IV. Testimony of Muss

1. Best evidence rule — Rule 1002   Although Muss testified that he took movies of Sonny and did not offer the movies into evidence, because the contents of the movie were events that Muss observed with his own eyes, his testimony is not subject to the best evidence rule. He testified about his personal, first-hand observations rather than about the contents of the movies. Thus, his testimony is not considered secondary evidence of the contents of a writing (although a movie meets the definition of a writing in Rule 1001(1)). His testimony is that he saw Sonny painting and playing and not just that he watched a movie that showed Sonny doing these things. Thus, the best evidence rule does not apply.

V. Testimony of police officer

1. Impeaching a hearsay declarant — Rule 806   The officer is recounting the out-of-court statement by Pagliacci. But is it being offered to prove the truth of the matter asserted? It is a statement that was made prior to the out-of-court statement recounted by Lucy Lips and is inconsistent with that statement. If Pagliacci's statement to Lucy is admitted through the excited utterance or statement against interest exception, then Rule 806 would apply. Rule 806 permits impeachment of the credibility of a hearsay declarant with a statement that is inconsistent with the admitted hearsay statement. So, it requires that some other hearsay statement already have been admitted. If Rule 806 applies, then the inconsistent statement is also admitted, regardless of whether it was made before or after the other hearsay statement that previously was admitted. Moreover, under Rule 806, the hearsay declarant is not required to be given an opportunity to admit or deny making the inconsistent statement.

VI. Evidence of use of screening filters

1. Subsequent remedial measures — Rule 407   Under Rule 407, evidence that remedial measures were taken after injury was caused by some event is inadmissible to prove negligence on the part of the entity who took the subsequent remedial measures. This evidence is admissible, however, if offered to prove something else, such as control or feasibility of precautionary measures. So, this evidence would not be admissible to prove the club's negligence. But because the club offered the testimony of the manufacturer's representative of the unfeasibility of precautionary measures, the evidence would be admitted to contradict that testimony and establish the feasibility of precautionary measures.

QUESTION #2

I. Testimony of Fred

1. Definition of hearsay — Rule 801(c)   Fred is testifying to out-of-court statements by the plaintiff. But these are operative facts, i.e., they are offered simply to prove that they were made and not to establish the truth of their contents. Consequently, this is not hearsay.

2. Admission — Rule 801(d)(2)(A)   Even if this out-of-court statement is offered to prove the truth of the matter asserted, it was a statement by the plaintiff offered against the plaintiff and so constitutes an admission under Rule 801(d)(2)(A) and is deemed not hearsay.

3. Offers of compromise — Rule 408   All statements regarding a claim that are made during settlement (compromise) negotiations, not just the offer of settlement itself, are inadmissible to establish the validity or amount of the underlying claim under the terms of Rule 408. Thus, all these statements would be excluded even if they are not hearsay as they all relate to the claim. And there was a "claim" because the statements were made at a settlement conference held after the complaint was filed.

QUESTION #3

I. Doctor's report

1. Hearsay within hearsay — Rule 805   This report involves double hearsay or hearsay within hearsay. The report itself is an out-of-court statement because Rule 801(a) defines "statement" for hearsay purposes to be a written or oral assertion, and it is being used to prove the truth of the matter asserted therein. The contents of the report include the doctor's recounting of what he heard his patient Karl tell him. This is also an out-of-court statement offered to prove the truth of what Karl told the doctor. Under Rule 805, each of these hearsay statements must fall within an exception for the report to be admitted.

2. Business records exception — Rule 803(6)   The doctor's report fits within the business records exception of Rule 803(6) because it is the type of report that is regularly produced in the normal course of his business. For it to be admitted under this exception, however, the proponent must offer evidence from a custodian or other qualified witness that this sort of record was kept in the course of a regularly conducted business activity, that it was the regular practice of the doctor's office to make such reports, and that it was made at or near the time the doctor interviewed his patient. If all of these foundation facts are established, the exception will apply.

3. Statement for medical treatment or diagnosis — Rule 803(4)   The patient told the doctor of his history of heart trouble. That statement of past medical history is admissible under this exception because it was relevant to the doctor's providing a diagnosis of and treatment for his current situation. The statement to the doctor that Lucy's negligence was the cause of the injury does not appear to be relevant to the doctor's diagnosis or treatment, however, and so would not fall within this exception. Thus, that part of the statement would be inadmissible.

QUESTION #4

I. Testimony of Pigeon

1. Character evidence — Rule 404   Evidence of the character of a non-witness in a civil action offered for the circumstantial purpose of proving that he acted in conformity with that character trait is inadmissible under Rule 404, regardless of the fact that it comes in the form of otherwise admissible reputation evidence. Thus, this testimony is inadmissible character evidence because it concerns the defendant in a civil case who did not take the stand as a witness.

2. Habit evidence — Rule 406   Under Rule 406, evidence of a person's habit or routine practice, regardless of whether or not it is corroborated, is admissible (unlike character evidence) to establish that the person acted consistently with that habit. To constitute habit, the conduct must be a routine response to a frequently occurring stimulus. But the fact that the witness characterized this as a habit is not dispositive. This is not the type of unthinking response to a frequently repetitive stimulus that would fall within the habit exception.

II. Grand larceny conviction

1. Impeachment of witness through extrinsic evidence — Rules 608(b), 609(a)(1), 609(a)(2)   Rule 608(b) provides that a witness's credibility cannot be attacked through extrinsic evidence of that witness's prior bad acts unless it meets the requirements of a conviction under the terms of Rule 609. Laurence did testify as a witness, so his credibility is subject to attack, and extrinsic evidence of his character for untruthfulness could be admitted in the form of a criminal conviction if it meets the requirements of Rule 609. Because the conviction is for larceny, this is not a *crimen falsi* (crime involving dishonesty or false statement) within the meaning of Rule 609(a)(2). It is, however, a felony punishable by more than one year under Rule 609(a)(1). Thus, it is admissible, and because the witness Laurence is not a criminal defendant, the trial judge does not have to engage in the balancing test set forth in Rule 609(a)(1), i.e., that the probative value of the conviction outweighs its prejudicial impact on the defendant. Rather, the judge is required to apply the test of Rule 403, i.e., determine whether the prejudicial impact substantially outweighs the conviction's probative value. Because the prior conviction was for stealing, and this civil case involves alleged conversion of property, the court might find that the jury will latch on to the prior act and use it as evidence that the defendant converted the plaintiff's property. If so, the court could find that this prejudicial impact (see discussion below of use of this as circumstantial evidence of character) substantially outweighs the probative value relative to impeaching the defendant/witness's credibility.

2. Character evidence — Rule 404   Prior bad acts cannot be offered in a civil case for the circumstantial purpose of showing that the actor acted consistently with the character trait reflected in those bad acts. Thus, Laurence's conviction cannot be admitted for the purpose of establishing that Laurence stole money from the plaintiff. It is admissible only for the limited purpose of impeaching Laurence's testimony as a witness.

3. Authentication — Rule 902(4)   The certified copy of the conviction meets the relevance requirement of authentication under Rule 902(4).

4. Best evidence rule — Rule 1005   The certified copy of the conviction meets the relevance requirement of authentication under Rule 1005, as it implements the best evidence rule codified at Rule 1002. That rule requires production of the original of a writing, when the proponent is offering to prove the contents of that writing. Under Rule 1005, a certified copy meets the original document production rule requirement.

QUESTION #5

I. Testimony of nurse Gimble

1. Definition of hearsay — Rule 801(c)   The nurse testified as to the conduct undertaken by the doctor. This would not constitute an out-of-court "statement" unless it is deemed to be assertive conduct, i.e., that the doctor intended to make a statement about the cause of the patient's problem by undertaking a particular form of therapy. If it is viewed as assertive conduct, then it would be deemed hearsay; however, that is an unlikely result because it is unlikely that the doctor was making a statement to the outsider world — he was simply treating his patient.

EVIDENCE LAW ESSAY EXAM #4

QUESTION #1

I. Testimony of Emil on direct examination

1. Opinion testimony — Rule 701   This is an attempt by Emil to offer lay opinion. There are two parts to this testimony: that the car was "flying" and that it was going faster than normal. The opinions will be admitted under Rule 701 as long as they are based on and are rationally connected to the witness's first-hand observation, are not based on specialized knowledge, and are useful to the jury. The "flying statement" meets all these requirements. It is useful to the jury because the jury was not there at the scene and could not have observed the speed of the car. But the statement that the car was going faster than normal is an opinion that detracts from the role of the jury. The jury needs to make that determination based on a less conclusory statement from the witness. So, that part of the statement would be excluded. Because the witness was not qualified as a streetcar expert, the statement that it was going faster than normal cannot be admitted as Rule 702 expert testimony based on specialized knowledge.

2. Agent admission — Rule 801(d)(2)(D)   Emil's testimony recounting the statement by conductor Bob repeats Bob's out-of-court statement and is offered to prove the truth of the matter asserted. Therefore, it meets the definition of hearsay. But is it an admission by an agent of a party? The plaintiff is suing the City and Bob is employed by the City and was making a statement relating to the course and scope of his job duties with respect to driving faster than usual and being behind schedule. Therefore, this part of the statement meets the definition of agent admission in Rule 801(d)(2)(D) and thus is deemed not to be hearsay. Bob's statement that the City was insured and would pay for Emil's medical bills is not within the scope of his agency, and so this part of the statement would not be imputed to the City and would not be an agent admission under Rule 802(d)(2)(D).

3. Liability insurance — Rule 411   Under Rule 411, evidence that a person was insured against liability is not admissible if offered to establish that the person acted negligently or otherwise wrongfully. On the other hand, Rule 411 also states that evidence of having insurance is admissible to prove agency or control. Thus, Bob's statement that his employer is insured is inadmissible to prove the City's negligence.

4. Offer to pay medical expenses — Rule 409   Under Rule 409, evidence of offering to pay medical expenses is not admissible to prove liability for the injury. So, the statement that the City would likely offer to pay the victim's medical expenses would be inadmissible under Rule 409 because it is being offered to establish the City's liability.

II. Testimony of Emil on cross-examination

1. Impeachment of witness for bias The Federal Rules do not expressly address the subject of the manner in which a witness can be impeached for bias. Consequently, we must look to the common law for guidance. Witnesses can be impeached for bias through the introduction of extrinsic or non-extrinsic evidence. Here, Emil testified and is being asked about his prior acts on cross-examination, so this is not an attempt to use extrinsic evidence. It is permissible inquiry on cross-examination of a witness as to the bias of that witness.

2. Character evidence — Rule 404 Evidence of prior acts offered, in a civil case, to prove that the actor acted consistently with the character trait reflected in the past act is inadmissible. Therefore, evidence of Emil's prior litigation history is not admissible to establish the lack of merit of his claim in this case, but it is admissible to impeach his credibility as a witness for bias.

III. Court records

1. Impeachment of a witness through extrinsic evidence The Federal Rules do not expressly address the subject of the manner in which a witness can be impeached for bias. Consequently, we must look to the common law for guidance. Witnesses can be impeached for bias through the introduction of extrinsic or non-extrinsic evidence. Here, after the witness denied the prior acts on cross-examination, the other side offered extrinsic evidence of those prior acts to show his bias against the City. That is admissible for the purpose of showing bias of a witness.

2. Character evidence — Rule 404 Evidence of prior acts offered, in a civil case, to prove that the actor acted consistently with the character trait reflected in the past act is inadmissible. Therefore, extrinsic evidence of Emil's prior litigation history not amounting to a conviction is not admissible to establish the lack of merit of his claim in this case, but it is admissible to impeach his credibility as a witness for bias.

3. Best evidence rule — Rule 1001(4) The defense offered a digital copy of court records to establish the contents of a writing. But under the best evidence rule, this is sufficient. The requirement of proving the contents of a writing with the "original" copy are met by offering a "duplicate" and a digitally created copy would meet the definition of "duplicate" contained in Rule 1001(4).

4. Authentication — Rule 901 Physical evidence must be authenticated to be relevant and admissible, i.e., evidence must be offered to establish that it is what it purports to be. Under Rule 901, authenticity can be established through any type of direct or circumstantial evidence from which a reasonable jury could determine that the object is what it is purported to be. Unless there is some reason to doubt the authenticity of this digitally created copy, the minimal requirement for authenticity will be satisfied.

IV. Testimony of Tom on direct examination

1. Definition of hearsay — Rule 801(c) The witness is recounting his out-of-court statement to the conductor, but it is not being offered to prove the truth of the matter asserted. Rather, it is being offered to prove that the statement was made to establish the City's knowledge of a problem. This is not a hearsay use of the statement and therefore it is admissible.

   2. Relevance — Rule 401   This evidence of a prior act similar to the act alleged in the complaint would be admissible as probative of the relevant issue of causation if the proponent of the evidence demonstrates that the prior act occurred under similar circumstances to those involved in the instant case. The fact that the statement was made two weeks before the alleged incident suggests a similarity of circumstances.

V. Testimony of Tom on cross-examination

   1. Impeachment of witness — Rule 608(b)   Under Rule 608(b), the witness Tom can be asked on cross-examination (i.e., not through extrinsic evidence) about any of his prior acts that go to his character for truthfulness to discredit his testimony. The question here, then, is whether having been arrested for gambling or prostitution or having been convicted of a vehicular misdemeanor goes to truthfulness. Certainly the misdemeanor convictions do not go to truthfulness. The alleged acts of gambling or prostitution may or may not, in the discretion of the trial judge. The fact that they are not convictions is irrelevant. Rule 608 allows in any evidence of alleged prior acts, and does not require a conviction.

VI. Testimony of Jane

   1. Rehabilitation of a witness — Rule 608(a)(2)   Jane is offering opinion testimony of witness Tom's character for truthfulness. This is an attempt to rehabilitate Tom's credibility, which can occur, under Rule 608(a)(2), only if his character for untruthfulness already had been challenged. The cross-examination of Tom did open this door, so rehabilitation is permitted; also, because this evidence took the form of opinion testimony, it is admissible under Rule 608(a).

VII. Testimony of Superintendent

   1. Impeachment of hearsay declarant — Rule 806   The witness Superintendent recounted the out-of-court statement by Bob. But Bob's prior out-of-court statement to Emil (that he had been driving uncharacteristically fast) was admitted under Rule 801(d)(2)(D), and so that testimony can be impeached by offering a hearsay account of a statement inconsistent with that statement. This statement is inconsistent with Bob's statement to Emil, and so is admissible to impeach the credibility of hearsay declarant Bob. Under Rule 806, the inconsistent statement can be made before or after the other out-of-court statement admitted under Rule 801(d)(2)(D).

   2. Agent admission — Rule 801(d)(2)(D)   The Superintendent's testimony recounting the statement by conductor Bob repeats Bob's out-of-court statement and is offered to prove the truth of the matter asserted. Therefore, it meets the definition of hearsay. But is it an admission by an agent of a party? The plaintiff is suing the City, and Bob is employed by the City and was making a statement relating to the course and scope of his job duties. Therefore, it meets the definition of agent admission in Rule 801(d)(2)(D) and is deemed not to be hearsay. It therefore is admissible to prove the truth of the matter asserted, i.e., the cause of his abrupt stop.

QUESTION #2

I. Testimony of officer Cleary — radio call

1. Definition of hearsay — Rule 801(c)   The officer is testifying as to what he heard out-of-court on the radio, but this statement is not being offered to prove the truth of the matter asserted. It is, rather, an operative fact, i.e., it is offered to prove that the call occurred. Thus, it is not hearsay and is admissible.

II. Testimony of officer Cleary — Steve's statement

1. Dying declaration — Rule 804(b)(2)   The officer is recounting Steve's out-of-court statement to prove the truth of the matter asserted therein. So, it is hearsay. Under Rule 804(b)(2), a statement made under fear of impending death that discusses the cause of the impending death is admissible; however, the declarant's statement did not concern the cause of his death, but rather, who was carrying the cocaine. So, it is not admissible under this exception.

III. Diary

1. State of mind — Rule 803(3)   The diary is a written out-of-court statement offered to prove the truth of the matter asserted therein and so it is hearsay. But it is also direct evidence of the declarant's then-existing state of mind, and so is admissible to show his statement of mind. Under the *Hillman* doctrine, the statement is also admissible to prove that the intent was carried out. That means it could be admitted to prove that the declarant participated in a big coke sale. And, most courts also admit it to establish that the other person mentioned in the statement, Ray, participated in the forecasted event.

2. Best evidence rule — Rule 1002   Under the best evidence rule, to prove the contents of a writing, the original of that document must be introduced. Because the original diary was introduced, this rule has been satisfied.

IV. Testimony of Louie — Ray's statement

1. Admission — Rule 801(d)(2)(A)   This is an out-of-court statement by the defendant offered against the defendant. It therefore is an admission and deemed not to be hearsay, and thus can be offered to prove the truth of the matter asserted as well as its impact on the listener, Louie.

V. Testimony of Louie — newspaper article

1. Definition of hearsay — Rule 801(c)   Louie testified to the contents of a newspaper article that he read. This is an out-of-court statement. But, it is being offered to prove its effect on the listener, i.e, circumstantial evidence of the listener's state of mind, and not the truth of the matter asserted. This is a non-hearsay use of the statement, and so it is admissible.

2. Character evidence of accused — Rule 404(a)(1)   The prosecution can offer evidence of an accused's character to show that he acted consistently with that character only after the defendant has opened the door by offering evidence of his good character. The defendant here did not open the door, and so the prosecution cannot offer evidence of his bad character through the reference in the newspaper article to his being an "enforcer" for the purpose of proving that the defendant acted in conformity with that character for violence in this case. Moreover, because the defendant Ray is charged with a narcotics offense, his character as a mob "enforcer" would not be evidence of a character trait relevant to the charged offense.

VI. Louie's diary

1. Past recollection recorded — Rule 803(5)   The diary is an out-of-court written statement being offered by the defense to prove the truth of its contents — i.e., to provide the defendant with an alibi that he was in another city on the date of the alleged crime. It can be read to the jury if the proponent establishes that the author had knowledge about the matter discussed in the diary and that he now does not remember its contents, but that the entry was made when the matter was fresh in his memory and accurately reflects that knowledge. If all of these foundational facts are established, the entry can be read to the jury. Here the defense counsel attempts not to have it read, but wants to have it received as an exhibit. Under Rule 803(5) it can be received as an exhibit only if it was offered by the adverse party. Louie was a witness for the prosecution and the defense is seeking to introduce the diary so this is permitted under Rule 803(5).

VII. Testimony of Louie on re-direct

1. Prior consistent statement — Rule 801(d)(1)(B)   Louie is recounting his out-of-court statement to the grand jury. This grand jury statement is consistent with his earlier testimony on direct examination that he and Ray had collaborated on the drug deal. Under Rule 801(d)(1)(B), this prior consistent statement made to the grand jury before trial is deemed not hearsay and admissible to prove the truth of the matter asserted if it is offered to rebut a charge of recent fabrication. The defense offered Louie's diary, which indicated that Louie had been in a different city than the city in which the alleged crime occurred. That was offered to impeach the credibility of Louie's incriminating statement, and so this prior consistent meets the test of Rule 801(d)(1)(B).

VIII. Testimony of Ray on direct examination

1. Character evidence of accused — Rule 404(a)(1)   Ray is testifying as to his prior acts to establish his good character. The defendant is permitted to offer evidence of his good character under Rule 404(a)(1) to show that he acted consistently with that character. That evidence must take the form of opinion or reputation, however, and not specific acts. This is evidence of specific acts on direct examination, and so it is inadmissible to prove the defendant's good character.

IX. Testimony of Ray on cross-examination

1. Guilty plea — Rule 410   Under Rule 410(1), evidence that a criminal defendant entered a guilty plea that subsequently was withdrawn is not admissible. Thus, the evidence of that guilty plea subsequently withdrawn (because Ray is being tried) is inadmissible. Similarly, under Rule 410(4), any statement made during the course of plea discussions with the prosecutor that resulted in a guilty plea that was later withdrawn is also inadmissible. Thus, the confession made during those nego-tiations is inadmissible as well as the fact of initially entering a guilty plea.

X. Testimony of Mary on direct examination

1. Character evidence of accused — Rule 404(a)(1)   The defendant can offer opinion or reputation evidence of his good character for the circumstantial purpose of proving that he acted consistently with that character in this situation. Mary is offering reputation evidence of the defendant's good character, and this is admissible under Rule 404(a)(1). The only question is whether this is evidence of a "pertinent" trait of character as required in Rule 404(a)(1). The reference to the defendant being law-abiding clearly is pertinent, but the reputation for being religious or being a family man is probably not pertinent.

2. Religious beliefs of witness — Rule 610   Because the defendant Ray testi-fied, his credibility as a witness can be challenged. Under Rule 610, however, evidence of the religious beliefs or opinions of a witness cannot be admitted to show that by reason of their nature the witness's credibility is enhanced. If, by offering opinion evidence of Ray's religiosity the defense was trying to rehabilitate the witness Ray's credibility, the statement would be inadmissible for that purpose.

XI. Testimony of Mary on cross-examination

1. Impeachment of character witness — Rule 608(b)   Mary has testified to the defendant's good character as being law-abiding. On cross-examination, under Rule 608(b), her credibility as a knowledgeable witness can be challenged by asking her if she knows of prior bad acts of the defendant that are inconsistent with what she said was his law-abiding character. Alleged past acts of armed robbery and child abuse would meet this standard, and so this evidence is admissible to impeach the character testimony of witness Mary. Technically, because Mary testified as to the defendant's reputation, she should have been asked whether she had "heard" rather than whether she "knew" of those past convictions. Courts rarely make that distinction, however, and allow "knew" questions when the character witness offered reputation, rather than opinion testimony.

2. Character evidence of an accused — Rules 404(a)(1) and 405(a)   Under Rule 404(a)(1), once the defendant has opened the door by offering evidence of his good character, the prosecution can offer evidence of the defendant's bad character to establish that he acted consistently with that bad character in the instant case. Under Rule 405(a), however, that evidence has to take the form of opinion or reputation, and here the evidence is of specific acts. So, while the evidence is admis-sible to challenge the credibility of the character witness Mary, it is not admissible to establish that the defendant acted consistently with a bad character to establish that he committed the crime for which he is charged.

EVIDENCE LAW ESSAY EXAM #5

QUESTION #1

I. Testimony of agent Claxton on direct examination about statement by defendant's attorney

1. Definition of hearsay — Rule 801I   Claxton is testifying as to an out-of-court statement by the attorney and it is being offered to prove the truth of the matter asserted there, i.e., that Jamison would accept a bribe in exchange for using his influence. Consequently, it meets the definition of hearsay, subject to the admissions exclusion from the definition of hearsay.

2. Representative and/or agent admission — Rule 801(d)(2)(C) & (D)   The statement by the attorney could be viewed as a statement by a representative authorized by the party (defendant) to speak for the party on this subject. But Rule 801(d)(2)(C) applies only when the party has expressly authorized the agent to speak on the subject in question. The facts here are a bit unclear about this. If there was an express authorization, then this constitutes a representative admission under Rule 801(d)(2)(C). As such, it is deemed not to be hearsay. Alternatively, if the attorney was not expressly authorized by the client to speak on this subject, the statement would be viewed as a vicarious admission by an agent because the statement concerns a matter related to the attorney's scope of employment, as the client asked the attorney to accompany him to the meeting (presumably for the purpose of representing his interests and speaking for him). As such, it would be deemed an agent admission under Rule 801(d)(2)(D) and therefore be deemed not hearsay.

3. State of mind — Rule 803(3)   The out-of-court statement reflects the present state of mind of a third party, i.e., the defendant. It does not refer to the state of mind of the declarant attorney. Consequently, it does not fall within the meaning of the hearsay exception codified at Rule 803(3) for declarations of present state of mind. Because the statement is not being offered to prove that it was made, but rather, that the third party to whom it referred (Jamison) would follow through with that intention, it is being offered to prove the truth of the matter asserted and is, therefore, excludable hearsay.

II. Testimony of Claxton about his reply to attorney statement

1. Definition of hearsay — Rule 801(c)   This is the witness's repetition of his own out-of-court statement. It is not being offered to prove the truth of the matter asserted, however, but rather that impact of that statement on the defendant/listener. Thus, the statement is itself an operative fact and the statement is not hearsay. Keep in mind, however, that the fact that the witness is repeating his own out-of-court statement does not preclude the statement, if offered to prove the truth of its contents, from being deemed to be hearsay.

III. Testimony of Claxton concerning Jamison's reply

1. Definition of hearsay — Rule 801(c)   Claxton's testimony repeats an out-of-court statement by the defendant that is being offered to prove the truth of the matter asserted therein, i.e., that he had done this sort of thing (influence peddling) before. Consequently, it is hearsay unless it is an admission.

2. Admission — Rule 8(d)(2)(A)   The out-of-court statement was made by the defendant and is being used against the defendant, so it is an admission and therefore not subject to the hearsay rule. It does not matter whether or not the statement is against the defendant's interests. All statements made by a party offered against that party are deemed admissions and not hearsay, so it is not inadmissible under Rule 802 (the hearsay rule). It could be excluded on some other basis (see below).

3. Character evidence of accused — Rule 404(a)(1)   The prosecution can offer evidence of the defendant's character for the circumstantial purpose of showing that he acted in conformity with that character and committed the charged crime BUT only, per Rule 404(a)(1), after the defendant has opened the door by offering evidence of his good character. Because the defendant has not offered evidence of his good character, evidence of the defendant's bad character is inadmissible. Moreover, under Rule 405(a), even if the defendant had opened the door, the prosecution could only come forward with evidence in the form of opinion and reputation, and here it comes in the form of specific acts evidence. So, it is inadmissible to establish the defendant's character and action in conformity with that character.

IV. Testimony of agent Bresh of his belief that Jamison is corrupt

1. Character evidence of accused — Rule 404(a)(1)   The prosecution can offer evidence of the defendant's character for the circumstantial purpose of showing that he acted in conformity with that character and committed the charged crime BUT only, per Rule 404(a)(1), after the defendant has opened the door by offering evidence of his good character. Because the defendant has not offered evidence of his good character, evidence of the defendant's bad character is inadmissible, even though it is in the otherwise permissible form of opinion evidence of character.

V. Testimony of agent Bresh about tearing betting stubs

1. Character evidence of accused — Rule 404(a)(1)   The prosecution can offer evidence of the defendant's character for the circumstantial purpose of showing that he acted in conformity with that character and committed the charged crime BUT only, per Rule 404(a)(1), after the defendant has opened the door by offering evidence of his good character. Because the defendant has not offered evidence of his good character, evidence of the defendant's bad character is inadmissible. Moreover, under Rule 405(a), even if the defendant had opened the door, the prosecution could only come forward with evidence in the form of opinion and reputation and this comes in the form of specific acts evidence.

VI. Testimony of agent Bresh about informant's tip

1. Definition of hearsay — Rule 801(c)   The statement by the witness relates to the informant's out-of-court statement offered to prove the truth of the matter asserted therein, i.e., that Jamison frequented prostitution services. So, it is hearsay and excluded under Rule 802 unless it falls within an exception (see below).

2. Declaration against interest — Rule 804(b)(3)   The statement is against the declarant informant's penal interest because he admits that he runs the prostitution service, which could subject him to criminal prosecution. Under Rule 804(b)(3), the declarant must be shown to be unavailable to take advantage of this exception and the proponent of the evidence (here, the prosecution) has the burden of establishing unavailability. There is no evidence here that the informant is unavailable, so this exception will not apply and the evidence will be deemed inadmissible hearsay.

3. Character evidence of accused — Rule 404(a)(1)   The prosecution can offer evidence of the defendant's character for the circumstantial purpose of showing that he acted in conformity with that character and committed the charged crime BUT only, per Rule 404(a)(1), after the defendant has opened the door by offering evidence of his good character. Because the defendant has not offered evidence of his good character, evidence of the defendant's bad character is inadmissible. Moreover, the nature of the character trait evidenced by these specific acts (which is also an impermissible form of character evidence) is not pertinent within the meaning of Rule 404(a)(1) to the influence peddling charge made against the defendant.

VII. Testimony by Jamison on direct — denial of taking bribes

1. Character evidence of accused — Rule 404(a)(1), Rule 405   The prosecution can offer evidence of the defendant's character for the circumstantial purpose of showing that he acted in conformity with that character and committed the charged crime BUT only, per Rule 404(a)(1), after the defendant has opened the door by offering evidence of his good character. This is an attempt by the defendant to open the door. Under Rule 405(a), that evidence must come in the form of opinion or reputation evidence; here, the defendant is offering evidence of (no) specific past acts. Specific acts are available on direct under Rule 405(b) but only if the character of the defendant is an element of the crime charged, which is not the case here.

VIII. Testimony of Jamison on cross-examination

1. Character evidence of accused — Rule 404(a)(1), Rule 405   The prosecution can offer evidence of the defendant's character for the circumstantial purpose of showing that he acted in conformity with that character and committed the charged crime BUT only, per Rule 404(a)(1), after the defendant has opened the door by offering evidence of his good character. This is an attempt by the defendant to open the door. Under Rule 405(a), that evidence must come in the form of opinion or reputation evidence; here, the defendant is offering evidence of (no) specific past acts. Specific acts are available on direct under Rule 405(b), but only if the character of the defendant is an element of the crime charged, which is not the case with the defendant's claimed fidelity to his wife.

IX. Testimony of Bornwell

1. Character evidence of accused — Rule 404(a)(1), Rule 405   The defendant can offer evidence of his character under Rule 404(a)(1) but, per Rule 405(a), only in the form of reputation or opinion testimony. The testimony by Senator Bornwell fits the requirement of being opinion, with a proper foundation having been laid by explaining how long the opinion witness knew the defendant. It is admissible.

X. Testimony of McDough about Bornwell letter

1. Impeachment of witness through prior inconsistent statement — Rule 613

Definition of hearsay — Rule 801(a)   The witness is testifying as to the contents of a writing, which meets the definition of a "statement" for hearsay purposes. But the witness's testimony is not being offered to prove the truth of the contents of the letter, i.e., that Jamison is a liar and a cheat. Rather, it is being offered to impeach the testimony of the witness Barnwell through the introduction of a prior inconsistent statement. Under Rule 613(b), the impeachment need not come out of the mouth of the witness sought to be impeached, but can be offered through extrinsic evidence as long as the witness is afforded an opportunity to explain or deny it. Most courts interpret this latter requirement as not requiring the witness to have been asked about the prior statement in advance, but that the witness merely be available for recall to explain or deny it. Under the common law, extrinsic evidence of a prior inconsistent statement by a witness is not admissible to impeach the witness if the prior statement is about a collateral matter. Rule 613(b) does not expressly codify this doctrine, but the trial judge could exclude the statement anyway under Rule 403 upon a determination that the prejudicial impact substantially outweighs its probative value for impeachment purposes. Although this case is about influence peddling and this statement concerns whether or not the defendant is a liar, because Senator Bornwell testified at trial that the defendant was an honorable person, his prior statement that the defendant is a liar is sufficiently probative to be admitted to impeach the credibility of the Senator's trial testimony.

2. Best evidence rule — Rule 1002, Rule 1004   Because the witness is testifying as to the contents of a writing, Rule 1002 is in play. It requires production of the original of the writing, rather than a witness's secondary evidence as to its contents. Under Rule 1004, however, such secondary evidence of the contents of a writing can be admitted upon a showing that the writing is unavailable, a showing that must be made by the proponent of the evidence. Absent such a showing, the secondary evidence is not admitted.

XI. Testimony of Claxton on Recall about instructions from boss

1. Definition of hearsay — Rule 801(c)
Hearsay within hearsay — Rule 805
Reputation exception — Rule 803(19)   The witness is testifying as to the content of an out-of-court statement made by his boss. It is hearsay if it is offered to prove the truth of the matter asserted therein, i.e., that Jamison was reputed to need money to pay gambling debts. If that is true, the statement is also double hearsay (hearsay within hearsay as defined in Rule 805) because the witness is testifying as to what the boss said others told him about the reputation of Jamison. That is relevant because it goes to the defendant's motive for committing the influence peddling.

The "outside hearsay," i.e., the statement by the FBI boss to "go after Jamison," is an operative fact and therefore is not hearsay.

The "inside hearsay" i.e., the statements by others to the FBI boss about Jamison's reputation, is admissible because of the hearsay exception for reputation evidence in Rule 803(13), which does not require the declarant to be unavailable. Thus, both parts of the statement are admissible.

2. Impeachment of defendant/witness — Rule 608   The defendant has testified, and so he can be impeached by offering evidence of his character for untruthfulness. But under Rule 608, this evidence must be offered in the form of opinion or reputation. This is reputation evidence, but the evidence must related to character for untruthfulness. The defendant's reputation for heavy gambling debts does not meet that requirement.

3. Character evidence of accused — Rule 404(a)(1), Rule 405   If this evidence is considered evidence of the defendant's bad character and if it is being used to prove that he was susceptible to bribery and so was bribed here, the prosecution can only offer such evidence though opinion or reputation evidence (which this is — reputation evidence), but only after the defendant has opened the door by offering evidence of his good character. The defendant's attempt to offer evidence of his good character was precluded because he offered it in the impermissible form of specific acts evidence. Consequently, if the defendant's good character evidence was excluded, the door has not been opened and the prosecution cannot offer evidence of the defendant's bad character if used to prove that he acted in conformity with that bad character in this case.

QUESTION #2

I. Testimony of Flast on direct examination

1. Definition of hearsay — Rule 801(c)

Hearsay within hearsay — Rule 805   The witness Flast is testifying as to the contents of an out-of-court statement made by the defendant and it is being used to prove the truth of the matter asserted, i.e., that he shot the victim. The statement also contains double hearsay to the extent the witness testifies as to what the defendant/declarant stated that Mark Pratt said. So, each statement needs to be addressed.

The witness's statement about what the defendant heard Pratt say (the "internal hearsay") could be viewed as not hearsay on the ground that it is being offered as an operative fact, i.e., not to prove the truth of the matter asserted (that there was an affair), but rather, the impact of hearing it on the defendant. Under this theory, that statement would not be hearsay. Because the "outside statement" by the defendant meets the definition of hearsay, however, we have to see if it falls within the admissions exemption and, therefore, is not hearsay.

2. Admission — Rule 801(d)(2)(A)   The hearsay statement was made by the declarant defendant and is being used against the defendant, so it is an admission and is therefore not hearsay. Thus, it is admissible and the internal statement is also admissible as not hearsay for the reason stated above.

3. Declaration against interest — Rule 804(b)(3)   Even if the out-of-court statement by Pratt is offered to prove the truth of the matter asserted, it could be viewed as a declaration against his pecuniary interests because it could subject him to civil liability for alienation of affection. This exception is available only when the declarant is unavailable, and the proponent of the evidence has the burden of establishing unavailability. Because there is no evidence that Pratt is unavailable, if the proponent cannot establish availability the exception would not apply. But, as stated above, Pratt's statement would not even fall into the hearsay rule or its exceptions if it is offered to prove the impact of the statement on the defendant rather than the truth of its contents.

II. Testimony of Flatt on cross-examination

1. Scope of cross-examination — Rule 611(b)   Inquiring as to the location of the witness when he heard the statements offered on direct examination falls within the scope of the direct examination as required under Rule 611(b) and so is permissible to ask on cross examination.

III. Testimony of Phillips

1. Definition of hearsay — Rule 801(c)   The witness is testifying as to the contents of an out-of-court statement made by the defendant and it is being used to prove the truth of the matter asserted, i.e., that he did not shoot the victim. Thus it fits the hearsay definition unless it is an admission (see below).

2. Admission — Rule 801(d)(2)(A)   The hearsay statement was made by a party — the defendant — but it is being offered by the defendant. Consequently, it is not an admission because under Rule 801(d)(2), a party's out-of-court statement is an admission only if it is offered against that party. So this is not an admission and, therefore, it is hearsay.

3. Excited utterance — Rule 803(2)   The statement by the defendant was made just after his argument with Jane. If the defense can establish that the defendant was still under the stress of the excitement caused by that argument, then the statement would fall within this exception if its contents relate to the startling event. But it is unlikely that the court would find that the declarant was still under the stress of excitement. Plus, the statement about not shooting her does not really relate to the exciting event — the argument. Thus, this exception will not apply.

4. State of mind — Rule 803(3)   The statement made by the defendant does not relate to his then-existing state of mind because he stated that his intention previously had been to kill Jane, and not his state of mind at the time he made the statement to witness Phillips. Thus, this exception does not apply.

5. Authentication — Rule 901   The witness testified as to the contents of a statement heard over the telephone. The fact that the voice was the voice of the defendant is a relevant issue and it must be authenticated. A witness's testimony that a voice heard on the phone is the voice of a person identified by the witness is deemed sufficient for identification assuming the witness has laid a foundation — i.e., established that she previously had heard the defendant's voice.

IV. Testimony of Wright about hotel register

1. Definition of hearsay — Rule 801(c),
Business records exception — Rule 803(6)   The witness is testifying as to the contents of a writing, which makes it hearsay if it is offered to prove the truth of the matter asserted in that writing, i.e., Flast signed in as a guest. Because that is what it is being used for, it is hearsay. Under Rule 803(6), however, a register is kept in the course of a regularly conducted business activity, and therefore it fits within the business records exception to the hearsay rule.

2. Best evidence rule — Rule 1002   The defense witness is testifying as to the contents of a writing, which is secondary evidence of the contents of that writing. The witness Wright did not testify that he remembered seeing Flast at the hotel, but that the register indicated that Flast had registered. Under the best evidence rule of Rule 1002, to prove the content of a writing, the original must be produced unless an exception applies, i.e., the original was lost, destroyed, or is unobtainable; is in the possession of the party against whom it is being used; or if it is not related to a controlling issue in the case. If, on the other hand, the contents of this writing go to a collateral matter, then under Rule 1004(4), the original document would not have to be offered. Flast had testified that he received a call from the defendant at his home in Miami on the morning of April 2. This testimony is offered to contradict that by showing that Flast was in San Diego the prior evening. Consequently, it is being offered to challenge the credibility of the witness Flast, which is not a collateral matter. Thus, the extrinsic evidence of the contents of the writing would be excluded under the best evidence rule.

V. Testimony of Wright about statement by Flast

1. Definition of hearsay — Rule 801(c)
Witness impeachment through prior inconsistent statement — Rule 613(b)
State of mind — Rule 803(3)   The witness Wright is testifying about the contents of an out-of-court statement by Flast. It will be hearsay if it is used to prove the truth of the matter asserted therein, i.e., that Flast planned to stay at the hotel. But since Flast, the former witness and now hearsay declarant, testified on direct examination that he was in Miami on the morning of April 2, this statement on the evening of April 1 that he planned to stay at the hotel in California for five more days is being used to impeach his credibility as a witness. Under Rule 613(b), this extrinsic (not coming directly out of the mouth of the witness) evidence of the witness's prior inconsistent statement is not admissible unless the witness is afforded an opportunity to explain or deny it.

The out-of-court statement by Flast is also being used to prove his then-existing state of mind and that he acted pursuant to that intention. As an expression of the declarant's then-existing state of mind, the statement is admissible under the 803(3) exception to the hearsay rule. And under the *Hillman* doctrine, it is admissible not only to prove the declarant's intention, but also that he followed through with this intention.

VI. Introduction of copy of deposition

1. Definition of hearsay — Rule 801(c)
Admission — Rule 801(d)(2)(A)
Former testimony — Rule 804(b)(1)   The defense is seeking to introduce an out-of-court statement made by the defendant at a deposition to prove the truth of that matter, i.e., that the defendant did not commit the murder. Thus, it meets the definition of hearsay. It does not constitute an admission under Rule 801(d)(2)(A) because although it is a statement by a party, it is not being used against the declarant as it is being offered by the defense. Consequently, it meets the definition of hearsay. One must then examine whether it fits within the former testimony exception of Rule 804(b)(1). Testimony previously given at a deposition fits within this rule but only if the party against whom it is now offered had an opportunity and motive to develop the testimony through cross-examination at that deposition. More importantly, the former testimony can be admitted only if the declarant is unavailable. Here the defendant is alive but does not want to testify. Under Rule 804(a)(1), the defendant is unavailable as a witness within the meaning of Rule 804 because he is exempt by Fifth Amendment privilege from being compelled to testify. So, the testimony would fall within the former testimony exception assuming the prosecution had an opportunity to cross-examine him during the deposition, which is likely the case.

2. Best evidence rule — Rule 1002   The defense offered a copy of the deposition. Under Rule 1003, a duplicate is admissible to the same extent as an original unless a genuine issue is raised as to its authenticity or using a duplicate would be unfair. Neither of those two situations exists here. The copy meets the best evidence rule requirement.

3. Authentication of physical evidence — Rule 901, Rule 902   Physical evidence must be authenticated to be relevant and admissible, i.e., the proponent must demonstrate that the document is what it purports to be. Since no evidence of authentication was offered, such as a certified copy of the deposition or a certificate of acknowledgement executed by a notary public or other authorized officer under Rules 902(4) or (5), it could be authenticated by extrinsic evidence from someone with knowledge of what it claims to be. Absent any such authentication, the deposition copy will not meet the authentication requirement.

VII. Introduction of certified copy of judgment

1. Authentication — Rule 901, Rule 902(4)
Best evidence rule — Rule 1001, Rule 1005   Physical evidence must be authenticated to establish that it is what it purports to be. Under Rule 902(4), no extrinsic evidence of authenticity is necessary for a certified copy of a public document. Because the defendant offered a certified copy of the prior judgment, the authentication requirement has been met. Offering a certified copy of this public record also meets the best evidence rule requirements of Rules 1001 and 1005.

2. Witness impeachment through evidence of bias   The defense offered a copy of a writing to prove the truth of the matter asserted therein, i.e., that the witness Flast had suffered a civil judgment at the hands of the defendant against whom he previously offered damaging testimony. This evidence is being offered not to prove the truth of the matter asserted in that judgment, but to impeach the witness Flast on grounds of bias against the defendant. The Federal Rules do not expressly address the subject of the manner in which a witness can be impeached for bias. Consequently, we must look to the common law for guidance. Witnesses can be impeached for bias through the introduction of extrinsic evidence such, as here, the existence of a civil judgment issued against them. So, this evidence is admissible for the purposes of impeaching the bias of witness Flast.

EVIDENCE LAW ESSAY EXAM #6

QUESTION #1

I. Introduction of six photos

1. Relevance — Rule 403   The photos are certainly probative of the manner of death, which is a material issue. And even one, or perhaps two, might not be so inflammatory that they would be excluded under the balancing test. Once we get to three, four, or more, however the trial judge will exclude these additional photos because the combined gruesome nature of the photos will inflame the prejudices of the jury and/or because the evidence has become cumulative and just wastes time. Therefore, some, but not all, will be admitted and those that are excluded will be excluded under Rule 403.

II. Sam's testimony that Ryper is violent

1. Character evidence — Rule 404   Under Rule 404(a)(1), the prosecution can offer evidence of the defendant's character for the circumstantial purpose of showing that he acted in conformity with that character and committed the charged crime, but only after the defendant has opened the door by offering evidence of his good character. The defendant has not "opened the door" to this evidence here and so the evidence of the defendant's bad character is inadmissible, even though it is offered in the otherwise admissible form of reputation evidence.

III. Sam's testimony about the theft conviction

1. Character evidence — Rule 404(b)   The prosecution is offering evidence of past act by the defendant. Rule 404(a)(1) prohibits the prosecution from offering character evidence of the defendant to show action in conformity with that character before the defendant has "opened the door" by offering evidence of his good character. Moreover, per Rule 405(a), even if the defendant has opened the door, such evidence can only be offered in the form of reputation or opinion and this is evidence of prior acts by the defendant. However, Rule 404(b) also tells us that past acts evidence is admissible if it is not being used to prove character, but something else. Here, the evidence of the prior robbery is not being offered to prove that the defendant is a thieving person (character), and so it is more likely that he committed the murder. Instead, It is being offered to prove that the defendant had the opportunity to commit this crime because he had possession of the murder weapon — the stolen sword. Therefore, the evidence *is* admissible. The fact that the prosecution offered the evidence in its "case-in-chief," i.e., before the defendant opened the door does not bar the introduction of the evidence under these circumstances because that rule applies only when the prosecution seeks to offer the evidence to prove character and action in conformity therewith. Under Rule 404(b), it does not apply when the specific acts evidence is offered to prove something else, such as opportunity or motive.

IV. Warren's direct testimony about Wanda's reputation

1. Witness impeachment — Rule 608   This is reputational evidence of a witness' character for violence. Rule 608(a) tells us that a witness' character can be admitted for impeachment purposes, but only through reputation or opinion testimony. This requirement is met. But the evidence also must go to the witness' character for truthfulness or untruthfulness, and this evidence of witness Wanda's violent character does not meet that requirement. So, the evidence is inadmissible.

V. Warren's direct testimony about seeing Wanda

1. Witness impeachment — Rule 608

Relevance — Rule 403   A witness' credibility can be impeached by offering contradictory evidence, but it is subject to the common law "collateral issue" rule. If the contradiction is offered via extrinsic evidence, it must contradict on a relevant issue. Here, the witness Wanda is being impeached by contradictory evidence that comes out of the mouth of another witness (Warren), i.e., extrinsic evidence of contradiction. Although the Federal Rules of Evidence do not contain an express rule barring impeachment through extrinsic evidence on a collateral issue, this "collateral issue" rule gets invoked by federal judges through an application of the balancing test of FRE 403, which permits exclusion if the probative value is substantially outweighed by, *inter alia*, considerations of waste of time. Because whether or not it was raining or sunny is not a material issue in the case, this extrinsic evidence of contradiction is inadmissible.

VI. Warren's testimony on cross-examination

1. Witness rehabilitation — Rule 608(a)(2)   Rule 608(a)(2) allows in reputation or opinion evidence of a witness' character for truthfulness (i.e., to rehabilitate, rather than to impeach, the witness' credibility), but only after reputation or opinion evidence of that witness' untruthful character has been offered. In other words, a witness's credibility cannot be rehabilitated until it has been challenged. Because Warren's direct testimony did not relate to Wanda's untruthful character, the prosecution cannot offer reputation evidence to rehabilitate her credibility as a truthtelling person as her credibility for truthfulness has not been attacked. So, this evidence is inadmissible.

VII. Louis's cross-examination testimony

1. Impeachment of witness through prior inconsistent statement — Rule 613(b)   The general rule is that a witness' credibility can be impeached through introduction of a prior inconsistent statement. Rule 613(b) even allows the prior inconsistent statement to be offered through extrinsic evidence, i.e., counsel is not limited to getting the witness to admit the prior inconsistent statement out of her own mouth. But the extrinsic evidence is admissible only if the witness is afforded the chance (either before or after the prior is introduced) to explain or deny the prior inconsistency and the opposing side (the proponent of the testimony of the witness who is being impeached) gets the chance to question the witness about the prior inconsistency. Here, because the witness was asked about his own prior inconsistent statement, there is no extrinsic evidence problem and so the answer is admissible for impeachment purposes. What this means is that if a witness is impeached through extrinsic evidence, that evidence is admissible only if the witness being impeached is still physically available to explain or deny it and to be interrogated about it by the counsel who was the proponent of the original testimony.

   2. Definition of hearsay — Rule 802   The witness Louis is testifying as to what he told a neighbor. This is an out-of-court statement. The fact that it is being repeated by the declarant on the witness stand does not remove it from the definition of hearsay. The evidence is not being offered to prove the truth of its contents, however — i.e., that Louis had been out of town on that day. It is being offered to impeach the declarant/witness's credibility. Consequently, it is not hearsay.

VIII. Dunn's direct testimony

   1. Character evidence — Rule 404, Rule 405(a)   This is character evidence of the defendant's peaceable character offered by the defendant to show that he acted in conformity with that peaceable character in a case where the defendant is claiming that he acted in self-defense. Under Rule 404(a)(1), the defendant can offer evidence of a "pertinent" character trait. But this evidence must be in the form of opinion or reputation evidence per Rule 405(a). This is evidence of the defendant's nonaggressive character used to prove conformity. Conformity is generally not permitted, but there is an exception for character of a criminal defendant when the trait is pertinent. The crime charged here (murder) is a crime of violence, and the testimony is about the defendant's nonaggressive character, which is pertinent; it is being offered by the defendant, and Rule 405(a) permits character evidence of a criminal defendant in the form of opinion or reputation. Here, the witness is offering his opinion of the defendant's character, so this is a permissible form of evidence and it will be admitted.

IX. Dunn's cross-examination testimony

   1. Form of character evidence — Rule 405(a)   The witness is being asked about past acts by the criminal defendant about whom he offered opinion testimony of character. Under FRE 405(a), the credibility of a witness' opinion testimony can be challenged by asking that witness about "relevant" prior acts of the person about whom he testified. So those past acts must be relevant to the content of the opinion testimony. Here, the opinion witness testified about the defendant's character for peacefulness or nonaggressiveness. Had the witness Dunn been asked about Ryper's prior acts of violence, that would have been OK. But Dunn was asked if he knew that the defendant had been convicted of tax evasion, a crime of stealing and lying that does not relate to aggressiveness. So this evidence is inadmissible.

X. Evidence of the felony conviction

   1. Impeachment of witness through extrinsic evidence of convictions — Rule 609(a)(1)   Because the defendant testified as a witness, his character for truthfulness can be impeached by extrinsic evidence of prior convictions under the terms provided in Rule 609. The general rule that a witness cannot be impeached on the grounds of character for untruthfulness through the introduction of extrinsic evidence does not apply when that extrinsic evidence takes the form of either a felony conviction or of a conviction of a crime involving false statement or dishonesty. The armed robbery conviction here does not fall within the Rule 609(a)(2) definition of a crime involving dishonesty or false statement, but it is a felony. Consequently, we must look to Rule 609(a)(1). Although the conviction meets the Rule's requirement of being punishable by imprisonment in excess of one year, there is a special provision applicable when the witness whose credibility is being impeached is the criminal defendant, as in this case. Under these circumstances, the Rule provides that the trial judge can admit the conviction only if the judge determines that the probative value of admitting this evidence outweighs its prejudicial effect on the accused. In other words, the presumption is against admissibility of any non-*crimen falsi* felony conviction of a witness who is also the accused. The defendant is accused of murder and this conviction is for armed robbery, an unrelated crime. So in one sense, its differentiation from the crime charged here suggests that its introduction will not unduly prejudice the jury. But an armed robbery conviction probably would be deemed to be of little probative value to establishing the truthfulness of the witness. Consequently, the prosecution probably has not rebutted the presumption against the introduction of this prior conviction and so it should not be admitted. Rule 609(b) also requires that the conviction not be more than ten years old (unless the judge determines that the probative value of an older conviction outweighs its prejudicial impact) and there is no evidence about this issue in the problem.

QUESTION #2

I. Ellen's direct testimony about repaving

1. Evidence of subsequent remedial measures — Rule 407   Under FRE 407, evidence of subsequent remedial measures is inadmissible to prove negligence, product defect, or need for warning. But it is admissible to prove something else, including ownership, control, or feasibility of precautionary measures if any of these matters are controverted. If the plaintiff is offering this evidence of the subsequent remedial measure to prove that the employer was aware that it had been negligent in maintaining its parking lot, the evidence is inadmissible for that purpose. Here, the supermarket claims that the parking lot is not under its control. This evidence, therefore, is admissible under Rule 407 to prove ownership or control.

II. Henry's direct testimony

1. Evidence of offer of compromise — Rule 408   There are two statements here. One is the offer of $30,000, and one admits that Ellen did not pay attention to the condition of the parking lot. The offer of $30,000 is evidence of a compromise offer and is excluded by Rule 408 as long as it is being offered to prove either the validity or invalidity of a claim or the amount of that claim, as long as either validity or amount is in dispute. And although the statement says that Ellen is offering the money only to make the case "go away," the fact that she is offering 60% of the amount sought in the complaint is certainly probative of her acknowledgment of the validity of Pete's claim as opposed to being merely an offer to avoid a nuisance. So, this is inadmissible. With respect to her other statement about not paying attention, the rule of exclusion in Rule 408 is broader than just the offer of compromise. It covers not only the compromise offer, but also any other statement made during the negotiations, including admissions of fault or other liability. These are sometimes referred to as "collateral statements of fact" and they, along with the offer, are excluded. So, this statement also will be excluded.

2. Definition of hearsay — Rule 801

Party admission — Rule 801(d)(1)(A)   The witness Henry testified as to an out-of-court statement made by the plaintiff that is being offered to prove the truth of its contents. But it is not hearsay because it is a statement made by a party that is being offered against that party. So under Rule 801(d)(1)(A), it is an admission and is therefore not deemed to be hearsay.

III. Charles's direct testimony

1. Evidence of liability insurance — Rule 411   Rule 411 excludes evidence of insurance or non-insurance, but only when that evidence is offered to prove wrongful conduct. Like other 400-level rules, if the evidence is offered to prove something else, such as control or ownership or bias, it is admissible for that purpose. The supermarket maintains that the parking lot is owned by the city. So because it is denying control over the parking lot, this evidence is certainly admissible to prove ownership or control of the insured premises. The evidence would be admitted for that limited purpose.

IV. Flora's tax return conviction

1. Impeachment of a civil witness through extrinsic evidence of a conviction — Rule 609(a)(2)   Although this witness was testifying in a civil case, that fact is not dispositive. Any witness's character can be challenged by evidence of a conviction as long as the evidence meets the requirements of Rule 609. FRE 609(a) divides convictions into two categories: (a) *crimen falsi* (crimes involving lying or dishonesty) and (b) others. Per FRE 609(a)(2), conviction of any crime, an element of which is lying or dishonesty, whether a felony or not, is admissible to impeach a witness' character. Period. Because false statement obviously is an element of the crime of filing a false tax return, it falls within the category of *crimen falsi* and so is admissible. The fact that this conviction is five years old means is not a problem, as Rule 610 excludes all convictions that are more than ten years old unless the judge finds that its probative value substantially outweighs its prejudicial effect. So, the fact of the conviction is admissible.

V. Flora's traffic offense conviction

1. Impeachment of a civil witness through extrinsic evidence of a conviction — Rule 609(a)(2)   Driving while intoxicated, unlike filing a false tax return or perjury, does not involve dishonesty or false statement. These are not necessary elements of that crime. Hence, this conviction does not fall into the automatically admissible category of *crimen falsi* under Rule 609(a)(2). Rule 609(a)(1) separates such convictions into two categories: crimes by a non-defendant witness and convictions of a witness who is also the defendant in a criminal case. Where the witness is not a criminal defendant, as here, convictions for non-*crimen falsi* misdemeanors, as here,

are not admissible. Thus, this conviction is inadmissible because it is a *non-crimen falsi* misdemeanor. If driving while intoxicated had been a felony, it would be subject to the rule that felony convictions of witnesses who are not the accused are admissible, except that the trial judge can exclude the evidence per Rule 403, i.e., if the judge determines that its prejudicial effect substantially outweighs its probative value. Thus, the presumption is in favor of admission of the felony conviction of a non-accused witness with the opponent of this evidence having to convince the judge that its prejudicial impact substantially outweighs its probative value. Because the facts here indicate that the conviction was a misdemeanor, is not a *crimen falsi*, and the witness is not the defendant in a criminal case, however, this conviction is inadmissible to impeach the credibility of the witness Flora.

VI. Flora's admission of lying in a prior lawsuit

1. Proof of character — Rule 405

Impeachment of a civil witness through past acts evidence — Rule 608   This is one of those situations that requires combining Rule 405's prohibition on the introduction of past acts evidence of character with the special 600 Rules for witnesses. Under Rule 405(a), even though evidence of the character of a witness can be offered, it must come in the form of opinion or reputation, subject to the limited exception in Rule 608. Rule 608 governs the admissibility of specific acts evidence, other than criminal convictions, relating to a witness' character for impeachment purposes. Rule 608(b) allows evidence of a witness' past acts, but only when offered during cross-examination of that witness and when it relates to that witness' character for truthfulness or untruthfulness. Here, the witness was asked about the past acts during cross-examination and those past acts relate to the witness character for untruthfulness. So, the exception of 608(b) applies and the evidence is admissible.

VII. Daniella's testimony

1. Hearsay within hearsay — Rule 805

Definition of hearsay — Rule 801

Agent admission — Rule 801(d)(2)(D)   The witness is testifying as to what he heard from a neighbor; the neighbor, in turn, is repeating what she heard someone else say. The neighbor's statement is an out-of-court statement that is being offered to prove the truth of the matter asserted therein, i.e., that a supermarket employee told him something. So, it is hearsay. However, the neighbor's statement repeats the out-of-court statement by the employee, and the employee's statement is being used to prove the truth of that statement, i.e., that this is not the first time a car had fallen into the hole in the parking lot. This is an example of what is generally referred to as "double hearsay" or, in the words of the FRE, "hearsay within hearsay." The first level of hearsay, often called the outside hearsay, is the neighbor's statement. The second level of hearsay, often called the inside hearsay, is the doctor's statement. Per Rule 805, for any of this to come in, each statement must separately fall within a hearsay exception or the combination of the two statements must fit within a hearsay exception. If that does not happen, both statements are excluded. To determine admissibility, we would need to determine whether both statements fit within an exception. The neighbor's statement is not an excited utterance (because there is no indication that the declarant neighbor was under the stress of excitement), dying declaration, present sense impression (the declarant was not describing an event while she was observing it), or any other recognized hearsay exception. So, it is inadmissible hearsay. The statement by the employee could be deemed an agent admission under Rule 801(d)(2)(D) if it concerned a matter with the scope of the employee's employment. That probably is not the case, because the declarant is a cashier whose job would not involve dealing with the parking lot. As it is not an admission, it is hearsay and does not fall within any recognized exception because there is no suggestion that the cashier was under the stress of excitement caused by Huggins's accident. Nor was the cashier describing the accident as it unfolded. Thus, it also is inadmissible hearsay.

VIII. Xavier's testimony

1. Definition of hearsay — Rule 801

Adoptive admission — Rule 801(d)(2)(B)   Xavier is repeating his out-of-court statement to Ellen. It is not hearsay, however, because it is not being offered to prove the truth of the content of that statement, but rather, its impact on the listener, Ellen. So, it is not hearsay. But the statement also contains a declaration that Ellen said nothing. Rule 801(d)(2)(B) includes within the definition of admission a statement that the circumstances demonstrate was adopted by the party against whom it is being used. This is an adoptive admission. This Rule typically comes into play when the party is silent in the presence of a statement that is offered against that party. The issue for the court is whether, under the particular circumstances, silence should be construed as adoption of the truth of that statement. Here, the defendant Ellen heard and understood the statement and it is reasonable to believe that this sort of statement, if untrue, would elicit a denial by the target of that statement. So it is an admission and not hearsay, and no other rule would preclude its admission.

IX. Dr. Jones's testimony

1. Definition of hearsay — Rule 801
Dying declaration — Rule 804(b)(2)
Definition of unavailability of hearsay declarant — Rule 804(a)
Present sense impression exception — Rule 803(1)
Excited utterance exception — Rule 803(2)   The doctor is testifying as to the truth of the out-of-court statement made by Shirley. So, it is hearsay. The declarant is unavailable as defined in Rule 804(a)(4) because she is dead. Rule 804(b)(3) provides an exception for an otherwise hearsay statement by an unavailable declarant when the statement is made under belief of impending death and concerns the cause or circumstances of what the declarant believes to be her impending death. Even assuming, which is not clear, that declarant Shirley was under a belief of her impending death, her statement about how Henry was driving does not concern the cause or circumstances of her impending death. Thus, it does not fit within the "dying declaration" exception and is inadmissible. It also does not fit within the present sense impression because she did not make the statement at the moment she observed Henry's

accident. Nor is it an excited utterance because her comment relates to his driving and there is no evidence that she was under stress caused by witnessing his driving.

X. Yolanda's direct testimony

1. Relevance — Rule 401   Yolanda's statement that the store had never received any notification of a problem in its parking lot may not be dispositive of the store's negligence, but it certainly is relevant as it is probative of that material proposition (notice relative to negligence) in the sense that it has some tendency to make the existence of that material proposition less probable than it would be without that evidence.

XI. Glenda's direct testimony

1. Best evidence rule — Rule 1002   The best evidence rule only applies when the proponent is offering extrinsic evidence of the contents of a writing. Here, the witness Glenda did not testify as to what the letter said, merely that it was received. Hence, the best evidence rule is inapplicable and the proponent need not offer the original of the letter but can offer testimonial evidence relating to its receipt. Proof that a writing exists or was received is not the same as proof of its contents.

Evidence Law
Multiple Choice
115 QUESTIONS

ANSWER SHEET

Print or copy this answer sheet to all multiple choice questions.

1.	A B C D	30.	A B C D	59.	A B C D	88.	A B C D
2.	A B C D	31.	A B C D	60.	A B C D	89.	A B C D
3.	A B C D	32.	A B C D	61.	A B C D	90.	A B C D
4.	A B C D	33.	A B C D	62.	A B C D	91.	A B C D
5.	A B C D	34.	A B C D	63.	A B C D	92.	A B C D
6.	A B C D	35.	A B C D	64.	A B C D	93.	A B C D
7.	A B C D	36.	A B C D	65.	A B C D	94.	A B C D
8.	A B C D	37.	A B C D	66.	A B C D	95.	A B C D
9.	A B C D	38.	A B C D	67.	A B C D	96.	A B C D
10.	A B C D	39.	A B C D	68.	A B C D	97.	A B C D
11.	A B C D	40.	A B C D	69.	A B C D	98.	A B C D
12.	A B C D	41.	A B C D	70.	A B C D	99.	A B C D
13.	A B C D	42.	A B C D	71.	A B C D	100.	A B C D
14.	A B C D	43.	A B C D	72.	A B C D	101.	A B C D
15.	A B C D	44.	A B C D	73.	A B C D	102.	A B C D
16.	A B C D	45.	A B C D	74.	A B C D	103.	A B C D
17.	A B C D	46.	A B C D	75.	A B C D	104.	A B C D
18.	A B C D	47.	A B C D	76.	A B C D	105.	A B C D
19.	A B C D	48.	A B C D	77.	A B C D	106.	A B C D
20.	A B C D	49.	A B C D	78.	A B C D	107.	A B C D
21.	A B C D	50.	A B C D	79.	A B C D	108.	A B C D
22.	A B C D	51.	A B C D	80.	A B C D	109.	A B C D
23.	A B C D	52.	A B C D	81.	A B C D	110.	A B C D
24.	A B C D	53.	A B C D	82.	A B C D	111.	A B C D
25.	A B C D	54.	A B C D	83.	A B C D	112.	A B C D
26.	A B C D	55.	A B C D	84.	A B C D	113.	A B C D
27.	A B C D	56.	A B C D	85.	A B C D	114.	A B C D
28.	A B C D	57.	A B C D	86.	A B C D	115.	A B C D
29.	A B C D	58.	A B C D	87.	A B C D		

EVIDENCE LAW QUESTIONS

Questions 1-14 deal with the following situation:

In a sexual harassment suit, Mary brought a claim under the federal civil rights statute against her employer and a state law tort claim alleging intentional infliction of emotional distress against her supervisor, John. Mary alleged that John subjected her to a barrage of unwanted sexual remarks and proposals that rendered her working environment hostile and abusive and caused her serious emotional distress.

1. To establish the company's liability for negligently failing to prevent or to remedy John's conduct, Mary's testimony that in the midst of this pattern of conduct by John, she informed Louise, the company Human Resources Officer, of the specific details of John's actions and comments is:

   A) not hearsay because it is an admission;

   B) inadmissible hearsay;

   C) not hearsay because it is not offered to prove the truth of the matter asserted; or

   D) hearsay but admissible under the former testimony exception.

2. Mary's testimony that Louise, the Human Resources Officer, told her, "this was unacceptable behavior and we will take care of it" is:

   A) inadmissible hearsay;

   B) not hearsay because it is an admission;

   C) not hearsay because it is offered to prove Louise's state of mind; or

   D) hearsay but within the exception for employee admissions.

3. The testimony of Jane, Mary's friend, that Mary coolly had told her of the specific acts and comments by the supervisor, is:

   A) irrelevant;

   B) not hearsay because it is an admission;

   C) hearsay but within the excited utterance exception; or

   D) inadmissible hearsay.

4. The testimony of employee Theresa that supervisor John had subjected Theresa to three other acts of harassment over the past year is:

   A) inadmissible per Rule 404(a);

   B) inadmissible per Rule 412;

C) admissible per Rule 415; or

D) admissible as nonhearsay.

5. To prove that he did not intend to cause Mary any harm, John's testimony that Jane, Mary's friend, had told John that Mary was very attracted to him is:

A) inadmissible hearsay;

B) not hearsay because it is not offered to prove the truth of the matter asserted;

C) not hearsay because it is an admission; or

D) hearsay but admissible under the state of mind exception.

6. To prove that John committed the alleged acts of harassment, a letter written by John to his best friend, Louie, that "I have this really attractive employee, Mary, working for me and I intend to have a sexual relationship with her, no matter what" is:

A) inadmissible hearsay;

B) not hearsay because it is a letter and not an oral statement;

C) hearsay but admissible under the state of mind exception; or

D) not hearsay because it is a statement against interest.

7. Testimony by Louise, the Human Resources Officer, that one day in the cafeteria, when John walked into the room, Louise saw Mary and Theresa look at John, burst into tears, and run out of the room is:

A) not hearsay because she is testifying as to her observations;

B) inadmissible character evidence;

C) hearsay because it is assertive conduct; or

D) not hearsay because it is an admission.

8. Testimony by Louise, the Human Resources Officer, that when she confronted John with all of Mary's charges, he smiled and said nothing is:

A) not hearsay because she is reporting what she saw;

B) hearsay because it constitutes assertive conduct;

C) admissible hearsay because it is a statement against interest; or

D) not hearsay because it is an admission.

9. After testifying that he never did any of the things alleged by Mary, John's statement on cross-examination by Mary's attorney that when confronted with

Mary's charges by Louise, the Human Resources Officer, in Louise's office, John stated, "Yes, I did proposition her on several occasions, but only because I really was in love with her," is

A) inadmissible hearsay;

B) not hearsay because it is a prior inconsistent statement;

C) hearsay but admissible under the former testimony exception; or

D) not hearsay.

10. After testifying on direct examination that she had seen John engage in sexual banter with Mary, a portion of Louise's deposition testimony that is read to the jury in which Louise stated, "I saw John walk into Mary's office and commit a very profane act in her presence," is

A) inadmissible hearsay;

B) not hearsay because Louise is reporting what she saw;

C) not hearsay because it is a prior consistent statement; or

D) hearsay but admissible under the former testimony exception.

11. After testifying on direct examination that Louise had seen John engage in sexual banter with Mary, in response to a question on cross-examination by John's attorney, Louise's testimony that she privately had confided to John before trial that she thought Louise had fabricated all of these charges is:

A) irrelevant;

B) inadmissible hearsay;

C) hearsay but admissible under the present sense impression exception; or

D) admissible to impeach Louise's credibility.

12. After Louise, the Human Resources Officer, testified that Mary had informed Louise of her allegations against John, Mary's testimony that prior to trial, Louise had told Mary that John had told Louise that he indeed did sexually harass Mary is:

A) inadmissible double hearsay;

B) inadmissible as a hearsay recounting of an admission;

C) admissible as a statement against interest and admission; or

D) not hearsay.

13. After Louise, the Human Resources Officer, testified that John had confirmed that he had made several lewd sexual references to Mary and had touched her in

offensive ways, Louise's testimony on cross examination that John also said, "And I did it because she asked me to do it," is:

A) inadmissible hearsay;

B) not hearsay because it is an admission;

C) hearsay but admissible under the declaration against interest exception; or

D) not hearsay under the rule of completeness.

14. The testimony offered by Steve, John's best friend, that John had told him, "I believe she really likes me and wants for us to become physically intimate," is:

A) hearsay but admissible under the state of mind exception;

B) not hearsay because it is an admission;

C) inadmissible hearsay; or

D) not hearsay because it goes to John's state of mind.

Questions 15-32 deal with the following situation:

Bill and Tom are accused of conspiring to molest three young children — Peter, Anthony, and Christopher — and of molesting them. At their trial, several pieces of evidence are offered.

15. To establish Bill's guilt, a police officer's testimony that during intensive custodial interrogation, Tom stated, "Bill molested those kids," is:

A) hearsay because it refers to the accomplished act;

B) not hearsay because it is an admission by a co-conspirator;

C) hearsay but admissible under the statement against interest exception; or

D) not hearsay because it goes to the police officer's state of mind.

16. The testimony by Victor, the father of Peter, one of the three alleged victims, that upon returning home, Peter ran into his father's room, broke down crying, and whispered, "Tom and Bill brought me into a dark room and touched me in a bad place," is:

A) inadmissible hearsay;

B) not hearsay because it is an admission;

C) hearsay but admissible as an excited utterance; or

D) admissible under Rule 414.

17. The testimony by Charles, the 25-year-old cousin of Peter, that Tom had molested him two years ago is:

A) inadmissible character evidence;

B) admissible under Rule 414;

C) irrelevant; or

D) inadmissible hearsay.

18. The testimony of a 911 operator who testifies that she received a call from someone who said, "I was walking past a house when I heard someone shout and I looked in the window and saw one of the defendants force himself upon this young boy. I immediately ran down the street to the first public phone and called you," is:

A) hearsay but admissible under the present sense impression exception;

B) inadmissible hearsay because the caller had run down the street before calling;

C) inadmissible character testimony; or

D) admissible under Rule 414.

19. The testimony of a pediatrician that during his examination of Peter, Peter said that Tom had sexually assaulted him is:

A) hearsay but admissible under the statements for medical diagnosis exception;

B) inadmissible hearsay because this statement was not made for purpose of diagnosis;

C) admissible under Rule 414; or

D) admissible under Rule 413.

20. The testimony of a nurse in the hospital emergency room that Peter's mother came rushing into the hospital with her son screaming, "My son was just molested," is:

A) inadmissible hearsay because the statement was made by the mother;

B) inadmissible hearsay because the witness is a nurse;

C) hearsay but admissible under the statements for medical diagnoses exception; or

D) admissible under Rule 414.

21. The child psychiatrist who examined Peter testified that Peter had told him that he had been molested by a man who works in his school, but that the psychiatrist could simply not remember the man's name. The psychiatrist does report, however, that, as always, he took careful and copious notes of the patient's statements during the examination. Can the prosecutor have the psychiatrist read to the jury that part of his notes of that conversation that includes the name given by Peter of the man who molested him?

A) No, because it is hearsay;

B) Yes, under the doctrine of present memory revived;

C) No, because it is hearsay and the identity of the molester was not relevant to Peter's diagnosis or treatment; or

D) Yes, because the doctor no longer can remember the name and the statement was made to a psychiatrist.

22. If a proper foundation is laid, can the defense offer a copy of the airline tickets and boarding passes that indicate that both defendants had flown to Europe on the day in question?

A) No, because this is hearsay evidence;

B) No, because it is irrelevant;

C) Yes, because it is hearsay but admissible under the business records exception; or

D) None of the above.

23. Another of the alleged victims, Peter, lived next door to Steve. Steve testified that one day Peter, in a hysterical state, came running into Steve's house screaming, "I was just assaulted by Tom, one of the janitors in my school, while I was waiting for the bus to take me home." Peter died before Tom and Bill were put on trial. This testimony is:

A) inadmissible hearsay;

B) hearsay but admissible as an excited utterance;

C) inadmissible because its admission would violate Tom's Sixth Amendment Confrontation Clause rights; or

D) not hearsay because it goes to Peter's state of mind.

24. The third alleged victim, Christopher, had sought assistance from a psychiatrist. During their session, he described in detail the series of unwanted sexual advances made by Bill. The prosecution offers the testimony of the psychiatrist who relays the contents of Christopher's statements to him. This testimony is:

A) inadmissible because its admission would violate Bill's Sixth Amendment Confrontation Clause rights because the prosecution has not established that Christopher is unavailable;

B) hearsay but admissible as an excited utterance;

C) inadmissible hearsay; or

D) not hearsay because it goes to Christopher's state of mind.

25. The third alleged victim, Christopher, had sought assistance from a psychiatrist. During their session, he described in detail the series of unwanted sexual advances made by Bill. The prosecution offers the testimony of Christopher, who states, "During my session with Dr. Frank, I told him that Bill had touched me many times in bad places." This testimony is:

A) inadmissible hearsay;

B) inadmissible because its admission would violate Bill's Sixth Amendment Confrontation Clause rights because the prosecution has not established that Christopher is unavailable;

C) hearsay but admissible under the statements for medical diagnosis exception; or

D) not hearsay because the declarant is testifying.

26. The prosecution in the child molestation case offers the notes taken by a police officer who was sitting in the police station when Christopher, the alleged third victim, strolled into the building. The officer took Christopher into his private office and began interrogating him. The notes state that in response to the first question, a subdued Christopher stated, "One week ago, I was sexually assaulted by Bill, the janitor in my school." Christopher passed away before the beginning of the criminal trial. This testimony is:

A) hearsay but admissible under the public records exception;

B) hearsay but admissible under the business records exception;

C) inadmissible because its admission would violate Bill's Sixth Amendment Confrontation Clause rights; or

D) admissible because the declarant is dead.

27. At Bill and Tom's criminal trial, the prosecution offers the testimony of a police officer who states that Bill told him during the first interrogation

session that both he and Tom had molested these three young children. This testimony is:

A) admissible against Bill as an admission but inadmissible hearsay against Tom with a corresponding limiting instruction;

B) inadmissible because its admission would violate the Sixth Amendment Confrontation Clause;

C) admissible against Bill as an admission and admissible against Tom as a co-conspirator admission; or

D) inadmissible double hearsay.

28. At Bill and Tom's criminal trial, the prosecution offers into evidence the written confession of Bill made to a police officer in which Bill confesses that both he and Tom molested these three young children. This evidence is:

A) admissible against Bill as an admission but inadmissible hearsay against Tom with a corresponding limiting instruction;

B) admissible against Bill as an admission and admissible against Tom as a co-conspirator admission;

C) inadmissible because its admission would violate the Sixth Amendment Confrontation Clause; or

D) admissible because it is a written confession.

29. At Bill and Tom's criminal trial, the prosecution offered into evidence an edited version of the written confession of Bill made to a police officer, in which Bill confessed that both he and Tom molested these three young children. Everywhere it appears, the word "Tom" is blotted out so that it cannot be deciphered. This evidence is:

A) inadmissible because its admission would violate the Sixth Amendment Confrontation Clause;

B) admissible against Bill as an admission and admissible against Tom as a co-conspirator admission;

C) admissible against Bill as an admission but inadmissible hearsay against Tom with a corresponding limiting instruction; or

D) admissible because all references to Tom's name have been eliminated.

30. After the termination of the criminal proceedings, the parents of Christopher bring a civil action for damages against Tom for his tortious sexual assault and battery of their son. They offer the testimony of Peter and Anthony, each of who testify that Tom had molested them. This evidence is:

A) admissible habit evidence;

B) inadmissible prior acts evidence of character;

C) admissible; or

D) inadmissible because Tom did not offer evidence of his good character.

31. After the termination of the criminal proceedings, the parents of Christopher bring a civil action for damages against Tom for his tortious sexual assault and battery of their son. Tom offers the testimony of Angus, one of Christopher's classmates. Angus testifies that everyone in school says that Christopher likes to initiate sexual conduct with adult men. This testimony is:

A) inadmissible hearsay;

B) admissible evidence of sexual predisposition;

C) inadmissible evidence of sexual predisposition; or

D) inadmissible because Christopher is a minor.

32. After the termination of the criminal proceedings, the parents of Christopher bring a civil action for damages against Tom for his tortious sexual assault and battery of their son. Tom offers the testimony of Lou, a teacher at Christopher's school. Lou testifies that he and Christopher have had consensual sex on several occasions. This testimony is:

A) admissible under the declaration against penal interest exception to hearsay;

B) inadmissible evidence of sexual predisposition;

C) admissible evidence of sexual predisposition; or

D) inadmissible because Christopher is a minor.

Questions 33-43 deal with the following situation:

Fred Jones is charged with robbing a bank in Los Angeles at 10:00 a.m. on September 1, 2008.

33. At Fred's trial in Los Angeles, Fred wants to offer into evidence the notes taken by a now-deceased police officer during the investigation of a robbery in San Francisco on September 1, 2008. These notes state, "I saw Fred Jones, who is known to me from prior run-ins with the law, running away from the gasoline station at 10:00 A.M. on September 1 with money falling out of his pockets." The police officer died before Fred's trial. This evidence is:

A) hearsay but admissible under the business records exception;

B) hearsay but admissible under the public records exception;

C) hearsay but admissible under the excited utterance exceptions; or

D) admissible because to exclude it would violate the defendant's Sixth Amendment right of confrontation.

34. Before the beginning of Fred Jones' bank robbery trial, a teller at that bank disappeared and never was found. At the trial, the prosecution seeks to introduce the teller's grand jury testimony where he stated that Fred Jones had walked up to his window with a gun and demanded that Fred turn over all of the money in his till. That testimony is:

A) inadmissible hearsay;

B) not hearsay because it is a prior statement under Rule 801(d)(1);

C) hearsay but admissible under the former testimony exception; or

D) hearsay because the bank teller is still alive.

35. At his trial, Fred Jones invoked his Fifth Amendment right against self-incrimination by choosing not to testify. Instead, he seeks to introduce his grand jury testimony in which he denied any participation in the bank robbery. That testimony is:

A) hearsay but admissible under the former testimony exception;

B) inadmissible hearsay because Fred chose not to testify at trial;

C) not hearsay because it is an admission; or

D) not hearsay because it is a prior statement under Rule 801(d)(1).

36. At trial, the prosecution offers the testimony of the wife of the deceased bank teller. She states that moments before his death from a long but inevitably fatal bout with cancer, in the presence of the priest who was giving the teller his last rites, the teller whispered to her, "Honey, please make sure you take care of the kids and my mom and make sure that the guy who robbed me and my bank, Fred Jones, is convicted." That testimony is:

A) hearsay but admissible as a dying declaration;

B) hearsay because the wife is available for cross examination;

C) hearsay because Jones is charged with bank robbery; or

D) not hearsay because it goes to the bank teller's state of mind.

37. At trial, in response to the defendant's denial of having committed the offense charged, a bank vice president testified that the reason there was no videotape of the presence of the defendant in the bank on the date in question is that he had ignored the report from his staff that the videotape system was not working and similarly ignored their urgent request to repair or replace it immediately. After Jones was acquitted, the bank's insurance company refused to reimburse the bank for the loss occasioned by the burglary on the ground that the failure to convict the robber and recover the money was the direct result of the bank's negligent monitoring of its videotaping system. The bank then sued its insurance company for unreasonable failure to pay in breach of the insurance contract. In its defense to that suit, the insurance company offered the transcript of the vice president's testimony at Fred's robbery trial concerning his failure to repair or replace the videotaping system after being warned about its failure by his staff. That evidence is:

A) hearsay but admissible under the former testimony exception;

B) not hearsay because it is a prior statement;

C) inadmissible hearsay because the insurance company was not a party to the criminal prosecution; or

D) inadmissible hearsay because the bank did not establish that the vice president was unavailable.

38. At trial, in response to the defendant's denial of the having committed the offense charged, a bank vice president testified that the reason there was no videotape of the presence of the defendant in the bank on the date in question is that he had ignored the report from his staff that the videotape system was not working and similarly ignored their urgent request to repair or replace it immediately. After Jones was acquitted, the bank's insurance company refused to reimburse the bank for the loss occasioned by the burglary on the ground that the failure to convict the robber and recover the money was the direct result of the bank's negligent monitoring of its videotaping system. The bank then sued its insurance company for breach of contract. In its defense to that suit, the insurance company offered the transcript of the vice president's testimony at Fred's robbery trial concerning his failure to repair or replace the videotaping system after being warned about its failure by his staff. The bank vice president died before the institution of the breach of contract action. The transcript evidence is:

A) hearsay but admissible under the former testimony exception because the vice president is dead;

B) not hearsay because it is a prior statement;

C) inadmissible hearsay because the insurance company was not a party to the criminal prosecution; or

D) inadmissible hearsay if the prosecution did not have the same incentive to cross-examine the vice president as the bank.

39. As part of its defense to the bank's breach of contract suit against it, the insurance company offers the testimony of the robbed teller's wife who states that moments before his death from a long but inevitably fatal bout with cancer, in the presence of the priest who was giving the teller his last rites, the teller whispered to her, "I told the vice president to replace the damned videotaping system." That testimony is:

A) hearsay but admissible as a dying declaration;

B) inadmissible hearsay because the bank teller died of cancer;

C) inadmissible hearsay because this is not a homicide case; or

D) not hearsay because it goes to the bank teller's state of mind.

40. During his pre-trial interrogation by the police, Fred Jones told the interrogating officer that he had extensive knowledge of the interior floor plan of the bank in question. At Jones's bank robbery trial, the interrogating officer testified about the interrogation session. The prosecution also offered into evidence the notes the officer took during that conversation. The note evidence is:

A) inadmissible hearsay;

B) hearsay but admissible under the public records exception;

C) hearsay but admissible under the business records exception; or

D) not hearsay because the police officer testified.

41. After the death of the robbed bank teller, his widow brought a wrongful death action against the tobacco companies alleging that her deceased husband's addiction to cigarettes was the cause of his fatal cancer. She testifies that moments before his death, in the presence of the priest who was giving the teller his last rites, the teller whispered to her, "Honey, go get those cigarette companies. I read a report from the Surgeon General's office just yesterday that they intentionally laced their cigarettes with an addictive level of nicotine and tar. The government is now convinced that it was these poisonous products that killed me." That testimony is:

A) inadmissible hearsay because this is not a homicide case;

B) hearsay but admissible as a dying declaration;

C) inadmissible hearsay because the statement is not based on personal knowledge; or

D) not hearsay because it reflects the bank teller's state of mind.

42. At the trial of Fred Jones for bank robbery, the defense introduces the testimony of the bank teller's wife, who testifies that moments before his death, in the presence of the priest who was giving the teller his last rites, the teller whispered to her, "Honey, after they convict that Jones guy, wait about six months and then go behind the swing set in our bank yard and dig up the suitcase I hid there. It contains the $1 million I stole from the bank." That testimony is:

A) inadmissible hearsay;

B) hearsay but admissible as a dying declaration;

C) hearsay but admissible as a declaration against his penal interest; or

D) not hearsay because it is an admission.

43. At Fred Jones' bank robbery trial, the only evidence offered by the defense is a statement by Wilbur, an inmate at the state penitentiary, who testifies that he heard his cellmate, Charles, boast that Charles had committed this bank robbery in Los Angeles on the morning of September 1, 2008 and that Charles was happy that his hated cousin, Fred Jones, was going to take the rap for a crime that he did not commit. Charles passed away before Fred Jones' trial. This testimony is:

A) inadmissible hearsay because it is uncorroborated;

B) hearsay but admissible as a declaration against Charles' penal interest;

C) not hearsay because it is an admission; or

D) hearsay but admissible as a declaration against Wilbur's interest.

Questions 44-47 deal with the following situation:

Sally is refused employment as an FBI agent because the agency determined that she was not an honest person who could be trusted with classified information. She claims she was not hired because of her race.

44. In her civil action against the FBI, Sally offers the testimony of a high school teacher who reports that she has known Sally her whole adult life and that Sally is an extremely honest, reliable, and thoroughly discreet individual. This testimony is:

A) inadmissible hearsay;

B) inadmissible character evidence;

C) admissible character evidence; or

D) admissible reputation evidence of character.

45. In her civil action against the FBI, Sally offers the testimony of her best friend, Lynn, who testifies that on three different occasions, she told Sally a highly confidential secret and Sally never revealed the contents of those conversations to a soul. This testimony is:

A) admissible character evidence;

B) inadmissible prior acts evidence of character;

C) inadmissible hearsay; or

D) none of the above.

46. In her civil action against the FBI, Sally also claims that she had been subjected to sexual harassment by the supervisor who conducted her interview. Sally offers the testimony of Laura, the FBI's Director of Human Resources. Laura testifies that she had been aware for some time that the supervisor who rejected Sally's application had been found to have sexually harassed other female applicants for employment with the Bureau. This testimony is:

A) inadmissible character evidence;

B) inadmissible hearsay;

C) admissible character evidence; or

D) not hearsay because it is an admission.

47. Sally decided to bring a separate lawsuit against the supervisor, Phil, asserting a tort claim for intentional infliction of emotional distress, alleging that his sexually harassing behavior during their interview had caused her severe emotional distress. Phil offers the testimony of another FBI supervisor, who states, "everyone in the Bureau thinks of Phil as a happily married guy who would never look at another woman." This testimony is:

A) inadmissible hearsay;

B) hearsay but admissible as an exception for reputation;

C) inadmissible character evidence; or

D) admissible evidence of a defendant's character offered by the defendant.

Questions 48-52 deal with the following situation:

Alice is prosecuted for criminal tax evasion.

48. The prosecution offers testimony of the defendant's reputation for being a cheat. This evidence is:

A) inadmissible character evidence;

B) admissible character evidence;

C) inadmissible hearsay; or

D) hearsay but admissible because it fits within the reputation exception.

49. Alice offers the testimony of her employer, who testifies, "Everyone in the shop says that Alice is as honest as the day is long." This testimony is:

A) inadmissible character evidence;

B) admissible character evidence;

C) inadmissible hearsay; or

D) none of the above.

50. Alice offers the testimony of her employer, who testifies, "On the few occasions when Alice arrives late for work, she always comes to my office to let me know that she was tardy." This testimony is:

A) admissible character evidence offered by the accused;

B) admissible character evidence because character is directly in issue;

C) inadmissible character evidence; or

D) admissible because it is the witness's direct observations.

51. Alice offers the testimony of her employer, who testifies, "Everyone in the shop says that Alice is as honest as the day is long." The prosecution then offers the testimony of Alice's neighbor, who testifies that he had caught Alice on three of four separate occasions stealing equipment from his garage. This testimony is:

A) inadmissible character evidence;

B) admissible character evidence because the defendant opened the door;

C) irrelevant; or

D) none of the above.

52. Alice's defense to the government's charge is that any mistake she made in her tax return was an unintended mathematical miscalculation. The prosecution offers the testimony of Alice's accountant, who testifies that for the past five years, Alice has instructed him to understate her income and create a home business deduction even though she does not work out of her home. This testimony is:

A) inadmissible specific acts evidence of character;

B) admissible because it goes to the question of Alice's intent;

C) inadmissible character evidence because the defendant did not offer any evidence of her good character; or

D) none of the above.

Questions 53-61 deal with the following situation:

Lee is prosecuted for the first-degree murder of his neighbor, Stan.

53. In support of his defense of self-defense, Lee offers the testimony of Sam, who testifies, "Everyone in the neighborhood knows that the deceased, Stan, was a very volatile and violent person." This testimony is:

A) inadmissible hearsay;

B) inadmissible character evidence;

C) admissible character evidence; or

D) none of the above.

54. In support of his defense of self-defense, Lee offers the testimony of a neighbor, Sam, who testifies, "Everyone in the neighborhood knows that the deceased, Stan, was a very volatile and violent person." The prosecution subsequently offers the testimony of another of Lee's neighbors, Karen, who testifies, "I have known the defendant, Lee, for more than ten years and he is a very violent person." Karen's testimony is:

A) inadmissible because the defendant did not place his character into issue;

B) inadmissible hearsay;

C) inadmissible because it is character evidence that is being used impermissibly to prove action in conformity with a character trait; or

D) none of the above.

55. In support of his defense of self-defense, Lee offers the testimony of a neighbor, Sam, who testifies, "Everyone in the neighborhood knows that the deceased, Stan, was a very volatile and violent person." On cross-examination of Sam, can the prosecutor ask whether or not he had heard that Stan had been convicted on two prior occasions of lying to a grand jury and perjury at trial?

A) No, because it calls for the introduction of hearsay evidence;

B) Yes, because it is a permissible use of prior acts evidence of character;

C) No, because it calls for the impermissible use of prior acts evidence of character; or

D) Yes, because it asks for the witness's state of mind.

56. In support of his defense of self-defense, Lee offers the testimony of a neighbor, Sam, who testifies, "Everyone in the neighborhood knows that the deceased, Stan, was a very volatile and violent person." When the prosecution subsequently offers the testimony of Greg, another of Lee's neighbors, can Greg testify that he saw Lee beat up two of his co-employees?

A) No, because it calls for the introduction of hearsay evidence;

B) Yes, because it is a permissible use of prior acts evidence of character;

C) No, because it calls for the use of prior acts evidence of character; or

D) Yes, because it asks for the witness's state of mind.

57. In support of his defense of self-defense, Lee offers the testimony of a neighbor, Sam, who testifies, "Everyone in the neighborhood knows that the deceased, Stan, was a very volatile and violent person." Can the prosecutor ask Sam on

cross-examination whether he had heard that on three different occasions Stan walked away from someone who had punched him in the face without so much as an unkind word?

A) Yes, because this is a permissible use of prior acts evidence of character;

B) No, because this is an impermissible use of prior acts evidence of character;

C) No, because this goes to the character of the victim; or

D) None of the above.

58. In support of his defense of self-defense, Lee testifies that the deceased, Stan, broke into his home, and came at Lee with a knife, threatening to kill him. The prosecution subsequently calls a witness who testifies that Stan is known throughout town as the calmest, most passive and peaceful person on earth. This latter piece of testimony is:

A) inadmissible hearsay;

B) inadmissible character evidence;

C) permissible use of character evidence; or

D) none of the above.

59. In support of his defense of self-defense, Lee testifies that the deceased, Stan, broke into his home, and came at Lee with a knife, threatening to kill him. The prosecution subsequently calls a witness who testifies that Stan was twice awarded the annual "Turn the Other Cheek Award" by his local house of worship. This evidence is:

A) inadmissible character evidence;

B) admissible character evidence because of Lee's testimony;

C) admissible because it is not character evidence; or

D) admissible because it does not relate to the defendant's character.

60. In support of its theory that Lee cold-bloodedly murdered Stan when Stan was sitting in Lee's living room watching television, the prosecution offers the testimony of Greg, who testifies that because he, Lee, and Stan had lived next door to each other for more than 20 years, Stan customarily walked into his and Lee's home unannounced and without knocking on the door. This evidence is:

A) inadmissible character evidence;

B) admissible habit evidence;

C) inadmissible hearsay; or

D) admissible character evidence.

61. In its case-in-chief, the prosecution offers evidence that Lee had stolen two handguns from a local sporting goods store one month before the alleged murder of Stan. This evidence is:

A) admissible non-character evidence if the appropriate foundation is laid;

B) impermissible use of prior acts to establish character;

C) permissible use of prior acts to establish character; or

D) inadmissible because the defendant did not place his character in issue.

Questions 62-70 deal with the following situation:

Lance is charged with committing a sexual assault upon his former wife, Loraine. He maintains that the pair did engage in sexual relations, but asserts that Loraine was a willing and aggressive participant in the alleged assault.

62. Lance wants to call three of Loraine's co-employees, each of whom will report that Loraine was their willing and aggressive sexual partner on several occasions. This evidence is:

A) inadmissible;

B) admissible under Rule 412;

C) admissible because it is not hearsay; or

D) none of the above.

63. Lance testifies that during their marriage, Loraine was always the initiator in their daily routine of sexual relations. This testimony is:

A) inadmissible evidence of prior sexual activity;

B) admissible evidence of prior sexual activity;

C) admissible habit evidence; or

D) irrelevant and therefore inadmissible.

64. Lance offers the testimony of one of Loraine's co-employees, who testifies, "Everyone at the office knows that Loraine is a very sexually aggressive person who loves rough forms of sexual conduct." This testimony is:

A) admissible evidence of sexual predisposition;

B) inadmissible hearsay;

C) inadmissible evidence of sexual predisposition; or

D) admissible because Loraine is the alleged victim.

65. Lance offers the testimony of one of Loraine's co-employees, who testifies that he has known Loraine for ten years and that she is the type of person who loves to initiate rough sex. This testimony is:

A) admissible evidence of sexual predisposition;

B) inadmissible hearsay;

C) inadmissible evidence of sexual predisposition; or

D) admissible because Loraine is the alleged victim.

66. In Lance's sexual assault prosecution, the prosecutor calls three witnesses, all of whom testify that Lance sexually assaulted them. This testimony is:

A) inadmissible character evidence;

B) admissible evidence of prior sexual offenses;

C) inadmissible because the defendant did not previously offer evidence of his good character; or

D) inadmissible hearsay.

67. In Lance's sexual assault prosecution, the prosecutor offers evidence that Lance had committed three armed robberies. This evidence is:

A) inadmissible prior acts evidence of character;

B) admissible because Lance is charged with sexual assault;

C) inadmissible because the prosecutor did not prove that Lance had been convicted of the armed robberies; or

D) none of the above.

68. At Lance's sexual assault trial, Lance's only defense is that he never engaged in sexual relations with Loraine on the day and time in question. He offers the testimony of his best friend, Sam, who testifies that he saw Loraine and Lance have sex on several occasions when Loraine, Lance, Sam, and Sam's then-wife were on vacation today in Paris one year before the alleged assault. This testimony is:

A) inadmissible evidence of prior sexual acts;

B) admissible evidence of prior sexual acts;

C) inadmissible hearsay; or

D) hearsay but admissible as a present sense impression.

69. At Lance's sexual assault trial, his only defense is that Loraine consented to their sexual activity on the date of the alleged murder. To challenge the truthfulness of Loraine's testimony that Lance assaulted her, Lance offers the testimony of

Virginia, who testifies that she and Loraine have been conducting a clandestine sexual relationship over the past three years. This testimony is:

A) inadmissible evidence of prior sexual acts;

B) inadmissible because it is not being used to establish the source of physical evidence associated with the alleged sexual assault;

C) irrelevant; or

D) admissible because exclusion of it would violate Lance's constitutional rights.

70. At his sexual assault trial, Lance's only defense is that Loraine was assaulted by someone else who had beaten her up during that assault. He offers evidence that Loraine had sex with her boss on the day in question. This evidence is:

A) inadmissible evidence of an alleged sexual assault victim's prior sexual history;

B) admissible evidence of an alleged sexual assault victim's prior sexual history;

C) inadmissible specific acts evidence of a victim's character; or

D) admissible because it goes to Lance's state of mind.

Questions 71-75 deal with the following situation:

Sam files a tort claim for damages against his employer, alleging that the company failed or refused to eliminate the presence of hazardous odors in the workplace and that Sam suffered severe medical and psychological injuries as a result of his continued exposure to those odors.

71. At trial, Sam offers the testimony of his co-worker, Amy, who testifies that she overheard several supervisors complaining about the odors and indicating that they hoped the company heard their complaints and did something about it. This testimony is:

A) inadmissible hearsay;

B) not hearsay because it is a declaration against interest;

C) hearsay but within the exception for admissions; or

D) not hearsay because it is an admission.

72. At trial, Sam offers the testimony of his co-worker, Amy, who testifies that she overheard several supervisors commenting that they were delighted that the company had heeded their complaints and removed the offending odors in the workplace. This testimony is:

A) inadmissible as evidence of subsequent remedial measures;

B) admissible because it is not hearsay;

C) admissible if offered to prove control or feasibility of precautionary measures; or

D) both b & c are correct.

73. Prior to trial, both parties stipulated that if the plaintiff could establish liability, the amount of Sam's damages would be fixed at $400,000. Prior to trial, Sam's lawyer met with the company lawyer to see if they could settle the case. During those discussions, the plaintiff offered to settle the case for $150,000. The settlement discussions were unsuccessful and the case went to trial. At trial, the company seeks to offer evidence of the plaintiff's $150,000 offer to establish the weakness of his claim of negligence and damages. This evidence is:

A) inadmissible hearsay;

B) hearsay but admitted under the admissions exception;

C) inadmissible because liability for the claim is disputed; or

D) admissible because the parties had agreed to the level of Sam's damages prior to trial.

74. Shortly after Sam filed his lawsuit, he was called into the office of the Director of Human Resources. At trial, Sam testifies that during this conversation, the Director said, "Listen Sam, I understand that you are upset about the odors, and we certainly should have done something about it earlier. But we were pre-occupied with other things. In any event, we want you to be happy at work and want to put all of this behind us. So we would like to pay for all of your medical and psychiatric expenses." The company objects to the introduction of all of these pieces of testimony other than the last sentence. How should the court rule on the objection?

A) Deny it because the statements do not refer to an offer to pay medical expenses;

B) Deny it because the other statement refers to psychiatric expenses;

C) Sustain it because this is hearsay; or

D) Sustain it because these are statements made in compromise negotiations.

75. At trial, the company offers the testimony of the Director of Human Resources, who testifies that she constantly patrolled the work area in which Sam and others worked on a daily basis. On cross-examination, Sam's attorney asks the Director if she is insured by the same company that insures the company and, if so, the name of that company. This testimony is:

A) inadmissible because it is irrelevant;

B) inadmissible because it is evidence that the witness and the company were insured;

C) admissible because the testimony goes to bias; or

D) admissible for all purposes.

76. Dave is indicted for the crime of sexual assault. During plea negotiations, Dave admitted to the prosecutor, "I sexually assaulted the victim." The parties ultimately agree on a mutually acceptable arrangement. The trial judge entered the guilty plea and Dave was sentenced. Thereafter, his victim brought a civil action for assault, battery, and intentional infliction of emotional distress against him. At the civil trial, the prosecutor testified as to the remark made to her by Dave. This testimony is:

A) inadmissible hearsay;

B) admissible because Dave pled guilty;

C) inadmissible as a statement made during plea negotiations; or

D) not hearsay because it is former testimony.

Questions 77-90 deal with the following situation:

Leon was charged with first-degree murder of a bartender in New York City. He insisted that this was a case of mistaken identity and that he had been visiting his sister in Pittsburgh during the time of the alleged murder.

77. After Leon testified on direct examination that he was in Pittsburgh with his sister on the date of the alleged murder, his lawyer called the sister, Lois, to the stand. Lois testified that her brother was with her during the time in question and that throughout his entire life she had known him to be incapable of telling a lie. The latter part of her testimony is:

A) admissible character evidence under Rule 404;

B) admissible character evidence under Rule 608;

C) inadmissible character evidence under Rule 404; or

D) inadmissible character evidence under Rule 608.

78. At the conclusion of the defense case-in-chief, which included testimony from Leon that he had been in Pittsburgh with his sister on the date of the alleged murder in New York, the prosecution offered the testimony of Charles Lane, a childhood friend of Leon's. Charles testified that throughout their childhood, Leon continually told falsehoods to his (and Leon's) schoolteachers and to all other authority figures, including, on three occasions, lying to his (Leon's) own mother. This testimony is:

A) admissible character evidence because Leon was the defendant;

B) admissible character evidence because Leon was a witness;

C) an inadmissible form of character evidence; or

D) none of the above.

79. At the conclusion of the defense's case-in-chief, which included testimony from Leon that he had been in Pittsburgh with his sister on the date of the alleged murder in New York, the prosecution offered the testimony of Charles Lane, a childhood friend of Leon's. Charles testified that Leon had been convicted of perjury on two prior occasions, with each crime punishable by imprisonment for no more than six months. This testimony is:

A) inadmissible because of the length of punishment set for perjury;

B) admissible only if the probative value exceeds its prejudicial effect to Leon;

C) an inadmissible form of character evidence; or

D) none of the above.

80. After Leon testified on direct examination that he had been in Pittsburgh on the date of the alleged murder in New York, the defense called Leon's sister, Lois, to the stand. Lois corroborated Leon's statement about his whereabouts on the date of the alleged murder. On cross-examination, the prosecution asked Lois if she knew that Leon had been involved in two armed robberies in the past. Defense counsel objected to the question. How should the court rule on the objection?

A) Deny it because this is cross-examination of a character witness;

B) Grant it because this is impermissible evidence of character;

C) Deny it because Leon was a witness; or

D) Deny it because these are criminal convictions.

81. After Leon testified on direct examination that he had been in Pittsburgh on the date of the alleged murder in New York, the defense called Leon's best friend, Fred. Fred testified that he had been out with Leon in Pittsburgh on the date of the alleged murder. During its rebuttal case, the prosecutor called Fred's friend, Bill, who testified that on the night of the alleged murder, Fred had called him and boasted that Fred had just seen Leon kill a bartender and that he expected that Leon would get away with it. Charles's testimony is:

A) inadmissible hearsay;

B) inadmissible extrinsic evidence;

C) admissible to impeach Fred's credibility if Fred is given an opportunity to explain or deny this statement; or

D) admissible to establish Leon's guilt.

82. After Leon testified on direct examination that he had been in Pittsburgh on the date of the alleged murder in New York, his sister, Lois, testified that she had been with him in Pittsburgh on the date of the alleged murder. The prosecution sought to offer a copy of Lois's grand jury testimony, in which she stated that Leon had told her that he had killed a bartender in New York and asked her to cover for him. This testimony is:

A) admissible to establish Leon's guilt;

B) inadmissible to establish Leon's guilt;

C) inadmissible to impeach Lois's credibility under any circumstances; or

D) none of the above.

83. Leon testified on direct examination that he had been in Pittsburgh on the date of the alleged murder in New York. During its rebuttal case, the prosecution called Leon's sister, Lois, who testified that she had been with him in Pittsburgh on the date of the alleged murder. The jury was unable to agree on a verdict and the prosecution decided to retry Leon. At the second trial, the prosecution once again called Lois and once again she testified that she had been with Leon in Pittsburgh on the date of the alleged murder. The prosecution sought to offer testimony of a police officer that after Leon's arrest, Lois had been questioned at police headquarters and had stated that she had seen Leon kill the bartender in New York. This testimony is:

A) inadmissible because Lois was a prosecution witness;

B) admissible to establish Leon's guilt;

C) admissible to impeach Lois's credibility; or

D) none of the above.

84. At Leon's trial, his sister, Lois, testifies that she and Leon were together in Pittsburgh on the date of the alleged murder in New York. On cross-examination, the prosecution asks Lois if anyone else can corroborate that fact, and Lois answers in the negative. On re-direct examination, the defense counsel asks Lois if she would lie just because Leon is her brother. She says no. Here answer is:

A) admissible because Leon did not testify as a witness;

B) admissible because Lois is being impeached;

C) inadmissible because Lois was not previously impeached for bias; or

D) inadmissible because this was not extrinsic evidence.

85. At Leon's trial, his sister, Lois, testifies that she and Leon were together in Pittsburgh on the date of the alleged murder in New York. On cross-examination, the prosecution asks Lois if anyone else can corroborate that fact, and Lois answers in the negative. The defense counsel then offers the testimony of Sam, Lois's neighbor, who testifies that he has known Lois all his life and that she is a very truthful person. Sam's testimony is:

A) inadmissible because Lois's character for truthfulness was not previously attacked;

B) admissible because this is opinion testimony of a witness's character for truthfulness;

C) inadmissible because Lois is not the defendant; or

D) admissible because this is not hearsay.

86. At Leon's trial, his sister, Lois, testifies that she and Leon were together in Pittsburgh on the date of the alleged murder. On cross-examination, the prosecution asks Lois if is true that she has perjured herself in previous court appearances. Lois denies making any false statements in the past. In its rebuttal case, the prosecutor offers the testimony of Mary, Lois's aunt, who testifies that on three occasions, Lois lied to her and her husband. Mary's testimony is:

A) admissible because it is an attack on Lois's truthfulness;

B) inadmissible because it is extrinsic evidence of prior acts by Lois;

C) admissible because Lois denied making false statements in the past; or

D) none of the above.

87. At Leon's trial, his former college roommate, Charles, testifies that he and Leon were at a movie together in Pittsburgh on the date of the alleged murder in New York. In its rebuttal case, the prosecutor offers the testimony of Frank, another college classmate of Leon's, who testifies that Leon and Charles were as thick as thieves in college and that Charles would do anything to help his buddy. Frank's testimony is:

A) inadmissible extrinsic evidence of a witness's character;

B) inadmissible extrinsic evidence of a witness's bias;

C) admissible evidence of a witness's bias; or

D) irrelevant.

88. At Leon's trial, his former college roommate, Charles, testifies that he and Leon were at a movie together in Pittsburgh on the date of the alleged murder in New York. In its rebuttal case, the prosecutor offers the testimony of Frank, another friend of Charles's, who testifies that for years before the alleged murder and

continuing up to the present time, Charles has been under psychiatric treatment for his extreme fear of heights. Frank's testimony is:

A) admissible impeachment testimony because Charles was a witness;

B) inadmissible hearsay;

C) inadmissible extrinsic evidence; or

D) irrelevant.

89. At Leon's trial for murdering a bartender in New York City, Peggy testifies that she and Leon went out for their first date on the day of the alleged murder, when they went to see a movie together in Pittsburgh. In its rebuttal case, the prosecutor offers the testimony of Charles, Leon's college roommate, who testifies that Leon and Peggy had been living together for years before the date of the alleged murder. Charles's testimony is:

A) inadmissible under the collateral evidence rule;

B) admissible impeachment evidence;

C) inadmissible extrinsic evidence; or

D) none of the above.

90. During the investigation leading up to Leon's trial, a police officer conducts an interview of Leon's neighbor, who tells the officer that Leon's parents died from the effects of alcoholism and that Leon has harbored a huge grudge all his life against anyone who profits from the sale of alcohol. When called to testify at Leon's trial about what possible motive Leon could have for murdering this bartender, the officer explains that Leon was motivated by a deep-seated hatred for persons who make money off of the sale of liquor. This testimony is:

A) admissible opinion testimony;

B) inadmissible opinion testimony;

C) admissible because of the witness's years of experience as a police officer; or

D) inadmissible hearsay.

Questions 91-100 deal with the following situation:

William is charged with the murder of his wife.

91. After retaining the services of attorney Paula to represent him in a murder prosecution being brought against him, William and Paula agree that William should plead not guilty by reason of insanity. During their initial conversation hours after the alleged murder, William described in detail how and why he had chosen to murder his wife. The prosecution seeks to compel Paula to reveal the manner in which William conducted himself during that conversation. Will Paula be compelled to disclose that information?

A) No, because it is hearsay;

B) No, because it is privileged;

C) Yes, because William asserted an insanity plea; or

D) Yes, because it is an admission.

92. After retaining the services of attorney Paula to represent him in a murder prosecution being brought against him, William and Paula agree that William should plead not guilty by reason of insanity. During their initial conversation conducted in William's cell, which he shared with another inmate, William described in detail how and why he had chosen to murder his wife. The prosecution seeks to compel Paula to reveal the contents of that conversation. Will Paula be compelled to disclose that information?

A) No, because the conversation was privileged;

B) No, because Paula and William created an attorney–client relationship during that conversation;

C) Yes, because Paula had not yet been hired by William; or

D) Yes, because of the presence of the cellmate.

93. After agreeing to represent William, Paula hired private investigator Steve to interview a variety of witnesses. After interviewing several witnesses, Steve reported back to Paula and William that all of the folks he interviewed had agreed to testify that William hated and had threatened to kill his wife. William then told Paula and Steve that he was not surprised; after all, it was true. He had planned to kill his wife for months. Can the prosecution compel Steve to report the contents of William's statement?

A) Yes, because Steve was in the room;

B) No, because the communication is privileged;

C) Yes, because it is an admission; or

D) None of the above.

94. During one of their many pre-trial conferences, William told Paula in confidence about a series of seven bank robberies that he previously had committed while he was in high school in Pittsburgh. After he was acquitted of murder, William and Paula jointly appeared on several TV interview shows regaling audiences with how they had so confused the jury about the real issues in the murder case that the jury never was able to convict William for the crime that he had committed. But William eventually became jealous of all of the

attention that was being lavished on Paula, and so he fired her. Some weeks later, on another TV interview show, Paula revealed what William had told her about six bank robberies that he had masterminded. She felt comfortable doing this because the statute of limitations for these six robberies had expired, and so William could not be prosecuted for them. When William was prosecuted for the seventh bank robbery, the prosecution sought a motion to compel Paula to testify at a deposition about the contents of the conversation between her and William with respect to this seventh robbery. The court will:

A) grant the request because Paula no longer is William's attorney;

B) grant the request because Paula waived the privilege by revealing confidences during the TV interviews;

C) deny the request because the prosecution has not established that the conversation is not privileged; or

D) deny the request because that information is privileged.

95. After committing the murder, but before his trial, William telephoned his wife, Marge, from whom he was separated, and told her that he was guilty. Marge was the one who sought the separation because of William's repeated acts of infidelity. William remained hopeful that they would reconcile and that Marge would move back into his home. Marge, however, was known by most of her friends to be happy to have broken free from an unhappy situation. Before trial, the prosecution informed the defense that it would be calling Marge as a witness. The defense filed a motion with the trial court to prohibit Marge from testifying in the case. The court will:

A) grant the motion because the pair is still married;

B) deny the motion because the statement is an admission;

C) deny the motion but prevent the wife from testifying as to the contents of the phone conversation; or

D) none of the above.

96. After committing the murder, but before his trial, William telephoned his wife, Marge, from whom he was separated, and told her that he was guilty. He also said that if she ever revealed what he said to a living soul, he would come after her and kill her. William is acquitted of the murder and is then prosecuted for the attempted murder of his wife. The prosecution calls Marge as a witness in the attempted murder case and asks her to reveal the threat made to her by her husband. The defense objects and asks the court to prevent the witness from answering that question. The court will:

A) preclude her from answering on the ground of spousal privilege;

B) permit her to answer because William is being prosecuted for attempted murder of the witness;

C) permit her to answer solely because this is an admission; or

D) none of the above.

97. After committing the murder, but before his trial, William telephoned his wife, Marge, from whom he was separated, and told her that he was guilty. He also said that if she ever revealed what he said to a living soul, he would kill her new boyfriend. After William was acquitted on the murder charge, he is prosecuted for attempted murder of the boyfriend. The prosecution calls Marge as a witness in the attempted murder case and asks her to reveal the threat made against her boyfriend by William. The defense objected and asked the court to prevent the witness from answering that question. The court will:

A) preclude her from answering on the ground of spousal privilege;

B) permit her to answer because William is being prosecuted for attempted murder of the boyfriend;

C) permit her to answer because the communication is not privileged; or

D) permit her to answer because the communication does not concern her.

98. The prosecution seeks to introduce into evidence the gun that it maintains that William used to kill the decedent. In advance of doing that, the prosecution establishes that a gun was found in the decedent's bedroom with blood on it and that this gun was taken to a vault in the police station immediately after being retrieved from the scene. It stayed in the station for two weeks, when it went to a laboratory for ballistics testing. At some point during the next three weeks, it was tested and the report was provided. How should the court rule on the defense counsel's objection to the introduction into evidence of this gun?

A) Sustain the objection because of the gap in the chain of custody while the gun was in the laboratory;

B) Overrule the objection because the gun's authenticity has been sufficiently established;

C) Overrule the objection because the gun had blood on it; or

D) None of the above.

99. When police officers arrived at the scene of the murder, they found a gun next to the decedent's bed with blood on it. The prosecution establishes that a gun was found in the decedent's bedroom with blood on it and that this gun was taken to a vault in the police station immediately upon being retrieved from the scene. It stayed in the station for two weeks, when it went to a laboratory for ballistics testing. At some point during the next three weeks, it was tested. Laura Ides, the ballistics tester at the laboratory, is called as a witness to testify as to the results of the ballistics tests she made on the gun that she examined. She will testify that the bullets from that gun match the bullets they found in the body of the deceased. The defense seeks to have the judge preclude Laura from offering that testimony. The court will:

A) not allow her to testify because the gun was not authenticated;

B) not allow her testimony because of the gap in the chain of custody while the gun was in the laboratory;

C) not allow her testify because that testimony is hearsay; or

D) allow her to testify and let the jury consider the gap in the chain of custody as a factor in determining how much weight to give to her testimony.

100. When police officers arrived at the scene of the murder, they found a gun next to the decedent's bed with blood on it. The prosecution establishes that a gun was found in the decedent's bedroom with blood on it, and that this gun was taken to a vault in the police station immediately upon being retrieved from the scene. It stayed in the station for two weeks, when it went to a laboratory for ballistics testing. At some point during the next three weeks it was tested by Laura Ides, a ballistics specialist. Laura prepared a report of her analysis of the ballistics examination of the gun and the comparison of that with the ballistic examination of the bullets taken out of the body of the deceased. At trial, she testified about the results of her ballistics investigation, all of which also happened to be contained in her report. The defense objects to her testifying as to the results of her ballistics investigation. The court will:

A) sustain the objection on the ground that the report itself is the best evidence;

B) deny the objection because the report is hearsay;

C) deny the objection if Laura is qualified as a witness; or

D) none of the above.

101. Frank is charged with murdering his next-door neighbor, Amanda. The prosecution maintains that Frank broke into Amanda's home, went into the kitchen, took a butcher knife from the kitchen, and went up to Amanda's room and slit her throat. The defense objects when the prosecution offers into evidence Amanda's decapitated head. The court will:

A) admit the evidence solely on the ground that it is relevant;

B) exclude the evidence on the ground that it is not relevant;

C) exclude the evidence because of its prejudicial impact on the jury; or

D) none of the above.

102. Frank is charged with murdering his next-door neighbor, Amanda. The defense calls four witnesses, and each one testifies that Frank is well known in the community for being a peaceable man who would never do harm to another living being. The prosecution objects to the testimony of the fourth witness. The court will:

A) admit the testimony because it is admissible character evidence;

B) exclude the testimony because it is inadmissible character evidence;

C) exclude the testimony because it is inadmissible hearsay; or

D) exclude the testimony on relevance grounds as being cumulative.

103. Jane filed a tort suit against Joe seeking damages that she suffered when he crashed his car into her car. In her case-in-chief, Jane offers evidence that Joe had previously been convicted for speeding on three separate occasions. This evidence will be:

A) excluded because it is being offered by the plaintiff;

B) excluded because this is a civil case;

C) admitted because Joe did not testify; or

D) none of the above.

104. Jane is charged with stealing documents from a neighbor's wall safe. In its case-in-chief, the prosecution seeks to offer evidence that Jane was convicted of robbing that neighbor's home of documents containing the wall safe combination. This evidence is:

A) admitted because it helps to establish opportunity;

B) excluded because it is an impermissible form of character evidence;

C) admitted because it is a permissible form of character evidence; or

D) excluded because its prejudicial impact does not outweigh its probative value.

105. Patricia, the defendant in a tort action brought against her after she crashed her automobile into the plaintiff John's home, testified that she lost her entire net worth two years ago as a result of poor investments and so she could never pay off any judgment rendered against her. She also testified that about a year ago she was forced to stop paying the premiums on her automobile insurance policy and, consequently, is no longer insured for any liability associated with this or any other car accident. The statement about her insurance policy will be:

A) excluded when offered to prove Patricia's negligence;

B) admitted because this is evidence of the absence of insurance;

C) admitted because Patricia does not deny owning or driving the car; or

D) none of the above.

106. After Patricia crashed her car into John's home, she was sued by John, John's uncle, and John's grandfather, all of whom were in the house at the time of the crash and all of whom were injured as a result of the crash. The uncle and grandfather settled their claims against Patricia. In exchange for receiving 20% of the damages they had sought in their suit, the uncle and grandfather agreed to dismiss their action and to testify against John in his remaining action against Patricia. On cross-examination, John's attorney asks the uncle whether it is true that he settled his claim against Patricia. The uncle answers in the affirmative. This testimony will be:

A) excluded because it is evidence of the settlement of a disputed claim;

B) admitted to establish the uncle's bias;

C) excluded because it is irrelevant; or

D) none of the above.

107. After Patricia crashed her car into John's home, she was sued by John, John's uncle, and John's grandfather, all of whom were in the house at the time of the crash and all of whom were injured as a result of the crash. The uncle and grandfather settled their claims against Patricia, receiving 20% of the damages they had sought in their suit. On direct examination, the uncle testifies, "During our settlement negotiations, Patricia admitted that she had been drinking large amounts of liquor immediately before crashing into my nephew's home." This testimony is:

A) inadmissible hearsay;

B) inadmissible because the statement was made during compromise negotiations;

C) admissible because the statement was not itself an offer of compromise; or

D) admissible because this hearsay statement falls within the declaration against interest exception to the hearsay rule.

108. One day after Patricia crashed her car into John's home, she called John on the phone and said, "I am so sorry for crashing into your home. I was really drunk when I was in the car and now I cannot sleep at night because of these tremendous feelings of guilt. Can you ever forgive me? I would feel a lot better if you would allow me to give you $25,000 for your trouble." Months later, John sued Patricia and, at trial, testified as to her telephone statements. This testimony is:

A) inadmissible because it is evidence of a compromise offer;

B) inadmissible hearsay;

C) admissible because it falls within the excited utterance hearsay exception; or

D) none of the above.

109. John sued Patricia for negligently driving her car into his home when she fell asleep at the wheel. At trial, Patricia offered the testimony of her sister, Sarah, who stated that Patricia is a very careful person who always gets plenty of sleep. John offers the testimony of Patricia's co-worker, Mary, who states that she once saw Patricia nodding off on the job. Mary's testimony is:

A) inadmissible character evidence;

B) admissible habit evidence;

C) admissible because Patricia offered character testimony by Sarah; or

D) inadmissible hearsay.

110. Shawn is accused of attempted murder by shooting a gun at his high school math teacher. At trial, the prosecution offers the testimony of Gail, another student at Shawn's high school, who testifies that Shawn previously had shot at his English and history teachers. This evidence is:

A) inadmissible because the evidence was offered by the prosecution;

B) admissible evidence of past acts for a limited purpose;

C) inadmissible habit evidence; or

D) inadmissible because Shawn did not offer evidence of his nonviolent character.

111. Thelma is being tried for possession of cocaine with intent to distribute. At trial, the prosecution offers the testimony of police officer Chris, who states that when he searched Thelma's home pursuant to a valid search warrant, he found a plastic bag full of white powder, that he immediately brought that package to the police laboratory, and that it was determined that the package contained cocaine. The prosecution then introduces a plastic bag filled with white powder that it claims was found in Thelma's home. How should the court rule on the defense objection to the introduction of this evidence?

A) Deny the motion because this is real evidence;

B) Grant the motion because it has not been authenticated;

C) Grant the motion because Thelma has not taken the stand; or

D) Deny the motion because the evidence is highly probative.

112. Thelma is being tried for possession of cocaine with intent to distribute. At trial, the prosecution offers the testimony of police officer Chris, who states that when he searched Thelma's home pursuant to a valid search warrant, he found a plastic bag full of white powder, that he immediately brought that package to the police laboratory, and that it was determined that the package contained cocaine. Dr. Evans, the forensic expert who tested the powder in the police lab, wrote up a report detailing his finding that the powder was cocaine.

At trial, Dr. Evans testified as to his professional qualifications and as to how and why he determined that the powder in the bag that he examined was cocaine. His report is not offered into evidence. His testimony is:

A) excluded because the report was not offered into evidence;

B) admitted because he testified from personal knowledge;

C) excluded because the real evidence has not been authenticated; or

D) excluded because he offered an opinion.

113. Dick is being prosecuted for robbing a store wearing a Dallas Cowboys uniform. The prosecution calls Witt to testify that he saw Dick run out of that store at the moment in question wearing a Dallas Cowboys uniform, but does not offer the uniform into evidence. The witness's testimony is:

A) inadmissible under the best evidence rule;

B) inadmissible because the uniform is real evidence that has not been authenticated;

C) inadmissible character evidence; or

D) none of the above.

114. Vernon is being tried for murdering his newspaper deliverer, Alicia. During the grand jury proceedings, Vernon's cancer-ridden cousin, Lamar, testifies that he drove Vernon to the scene, where he watched Vernon "whack" the deliverer. Fortunately for Lamar, his cancer went into remission after departing the grand jury room. At Vernon's trial, Lamar invoked his Fifth Amendment right against self-incrimination and refused to answer any and all questions propounded to him. So the prosecution offered Lamar's statement to the grand jury by introducing the relevant portions of the transcript of those proceedings. When the defense objects to the introduction of that testimony, the court should:

A) exclude the testimony pursuant to the constitutional Confrontation Clause;

B) admit the testimony because it falls within the former testimony exception to the hearsay rule;

C) exclude the testimony because it is inadmissible hearsay; or

D) admit the testimony because it was a declaration against penal interest.

115. Vernon is being tried for murdering his newspaper deliverer, Alicia. During the grand jury proceedings, Vernon's cancer-ridden cousin, Lamar, testified that he drove Vernon to the scene, where he watched Vernon "whack" the deliverer. Fortunately for Lamar, his cancer went into remission after departing the grand jury room. Unfortunately for Lamar, Vernon tracked Lamar down at an FBI safe house and yelled, "You'll never make it alive to that courthouse," as he shot Lamar in the head, killing him instantly. At Vernon's trial, the prosecution offered Lamar's statement to the grand jury by introducing the relevant portions of the transcript of those proceedings. When the defense objects to the introduction of the testimony, the court should:

A) exclude the testimony pursuant to the constitutional Confrontation Clause;

B) admit the testimony because Vernon ordered Lamar's murder to keep him from testifying at trial;

C) exclude the testimony because it is inadmissible hearsay; or

D) admit the testimony because it was an admission.

Evidence Law
Multiple Choice
ANSWERS & ANALYSIS

> ## EVIDENCE LAW ANSWERS AND ANALYSIS

1. Issue: Definition of hearsay

The correct answer is **C**. This out-of-court statement is not hearsay because it is offered to establish that the company was on notice of Mary's complaint and thereby liable for the actions of John. Answer B is wrong because Mary's testimony concerning her out-of-court statement to Louise was offered to establish that the company heard the statement through its representative, rather than to prove the truth of the statement itself. It is not hearsay. Answer A is wrong because this was not a statement made by a party that was used against that party. It was Mary's statement and it was offered against the company, not against Mary. Answer D is incorrect because the former testimony exception of 804(b)(1) only applies when the declarant is unavailable and the declarant is Mary who testified. Plus, her statement was not made at another "hearing" or in a deposition as required in Rule 804(b)(1).

2. Issue: Agent/spokesman admission

The correct answer is **B**. This out-of-court statement was made by the company's representative, and so it falls within an admission either by an authorized spokesman or an employee acting within the course of her employment under Rules 801(d)(2)(C) or (D). Answer A is incorrect because this out-of-court statement was made by the company's representative, so it falls within an admission either by an authorized spokesman or an employee acting within the course of her employment under Rules 801(d)(2)(C) or (D) and is therefore deemed to be not hearsay. Answer C is incorrect because it is not being offered to prove the declarant's state of mind, but is offered to prove the truth of the matter asserted. Answer D is incorrect because an employee admission renders the statement not hearsay under Rule 801(d)(2) and not within an exception to the hearsay rule under Rules 803 or 804.

3. Issue: Definition of hearsay

The correct answer is **D**. This is an out-of-court statement offered to prove the truth of the matter asserted and is classic hearsay that does not fall within any exception. Answer C is incorrect because this is not an excited utterance; Mary "coolly" told Jane about it. Answer B is incorrect because it is not being used against the declarant/party, as required under Rule 801(d)(2). Answer A is incorrect because the remarks of the supervisor are directly probative of the defendant's liability.

4. Issue: Circumstantial use of character evidence

The correct answer is **A**. This is character evidence being used circumstantially to prove that John acted consistently with this character trait in this case. Because John is neither the defendant nor the victim in a criminal case, nor a witness, none of the exceptions in Rule 404 applies and so the general rule of Rule 404(a) prohibiting the circumstantial use of evidence of character to prove action in conformity applies. Answer B is incorrect because Rule 412 only allows in evidence of past acts by the alleged victim and this is an attempt to offer evidence of the past sexual history of the perpetrator. Answer C is incorrect because Rule 415 only allows in evidence of prior sexual acts that constitute a sexual assault and the evidence of John's prior conduct does not. Answer D is incorrect because although this admission testimony is not barred by the hearsay rule, it is excluded under Rule 404(a).

5. Issue: Definition of hearsay

The correct answer is **B**. This out-of-court statement is offered to prove the effect of the declarant (Jane)'s statement on John's state of mind in terms of whether he thought that Mary would find his advances inappropriate or unwelcome. Thus, it is not hearsay because the statement is not offered to prove the truth of the matter asserted. Answer A is incorrect because the statement is not hearsay because it is not being offered to prove the truth of the matter asserted. Answer C is incorrect because the out-of-court statement was not made by a party, but by Jane, so it is not an admission. Answer D is incorrect because the state of mind exception to hearsay codified in Rule 803(3) applies only to statements that directly express the declarant's state of mind and not statements used circumstantially to prove the state of mind of the declarant or listener. Jane's statement was not an express articulation of her state of mind, let alone the state of mind of the listener, John.

6. Issue: State of mind exception

The correct answer is **C**. The letter/declaration is being used to prove the truth of the matter asserted, i.e., that the declarant John intends to have a sexual relationship with Mary. This is a classic state of mind statement because it expresses his intention. It is direct evidence of his intention. Thus, it is hearsay but it is subject to the Rule 803(3) exception. Moreover, under the *Hillman* doctrine, it is admissible not only to prove the declarant's intention but also that he followed through with this intention. Answer A is wrong because although the statement is hearsay, it falls within the state of mind exception of Rule 803(3). Answer B is incorrect because the fact that this out-of-court statement comes in the form of a writing would not prevent it from being hearsay as the definition of an out-of-court statement for hearsay purposes in Rule 801(a) includes writings. Answer D is incorrect because the statement against interest exception does not apply to statements by a party. Because John is a party, the statement can be an admission, but not a declaration against interest.

7. Issue: Assertive conduct as hearsay "statement"

The correct answer is **C**. An out-of-court "statement" for hearsay purposes is defined in Rule 801(a) to include nonverbal conduct that is intended by the actor to be an assertion. This is an example of such assertive conduct. Their conduct suggests that they are making a statement of how upset they are with John. It is therefore hearsay and does not fit within any exception. Answer A is incorrect because it ignores the possibility that conduct can be a statement for hearsay purposes. Answer B is incorrect because it is not evidence of John's character being used to show that he acted in conformity with that character trait. Answer D is incorrect because an admission is a statement by a party used against that party, and while Mary is a party (Theresa is not), the statement is being offered by them and not against them.

8. Issue: Admission

The correct answer is **D**. Rule 801(d)(2)(B) includes within the definition of an admission adoptive admissions, i.e., admissions that are imputed to the non-declarant when his silence in the face of a statement by someone else indicates adherence to that statement when a person normally would respond if they did not agree with the statement. And as an admission, such silence is deemed not to be hearsay. Answer A is incorrect because it ignores this concept of adoptive admission by silence or nonverbal conduct. Answer B is wrong because the fact that it is assertive conduct here goes to whether or not it is an admission, not just whether it is a statement for hearsay purposes. It is a statement; but a statement by a party offered against him, which constitutes an admission and, therefore, is deemed not to be hearsay under Rule 801(d)(2)(b). Answer C is incorrect because it is a statement by a party and so not a declaration against interest.

9. Issue: Definition of hearsay

The correct answer is **D**. This is an out-of-court statement offered to prove the truth of the matter asserted therein that does not fall within any exception. But it is an admission because it is a statement made by a party that is being used against that party. Thus, it is deemed not to be hearsay under Rule 801(d)(2)(A). Answer A is incorrect because this is not hearsay; it is an admission by a party used against him. Thus, it is deemed not to be hearsay under Rule 801(d)(2)(A). Answer B is incorrect because it is not a prior inconsistent statement within the meaning of Rule 801(d)(1) because the out-of-court statement was not made under oath subject to penalty of perjury at some other hearing or in a deposition. Answer C is incorrect because it is not former testimony as it was not offered at some other "hearing" or deposition as required in Rule 804(b)(1). Plus, this exception requires the declarant to be unavailable and John, the declarant, was a witness.

10. Issue: Definition of hearsay

The correct answer is **A**. This is an out-of-court statement offered to prove the truth of the matter asserted, and so it is hearsay. It falls within no exception. Answer B is wrong because the testimony is an out-of-court statement. The fact that the out-of-court statement (statement made during the deposition) refers to an eyewitness account does not make it not hearsay. Answer C is wrong because a prior consistent statement cannot be introduced into evidence under Rule 801(d)(1)(B) unless it is offered to rebut a charge against the declarant of recent fabrication. There was no charge that Louise had fabricated her trial testimony, and so she cannot offer a prior consistent. Answer D is incorrect because the former testimony exception in Rule 804(b)(1) can be used only when the declarant is unavailable. The declarant Louise was a witness.

11. Issue: Witness impeachment

The correct answer is **D**. Although this is an out-of-court statement, it is not being offered to prove the truth of the matter asserted, which means that it is not hearsay. Rather, it is being used to impeach the credibility of the declarant through her own prior statement. This non-substantive use of the statement renders it not hearsay. Answer A is incorrect because the statement is being offered for impeachment purposes. Answer B is incorrect because although this is an out-of-court statement, it is not being offered to prove the truth of the matter asserted, which means that it is not hearsay. Rather, it is being used to impeach the credibility of the declarant through her own prior statement. This non-substantive use of the statement renders it not hearsay. Answer C is incorrect because the statement is not hearsay and therefore need not fall within any exception to be admitted.

12. Issue: Double hearsay

The correct answer is **D**. This is properly analyzed as a double hearsay (hearsay within hearsay) problem. Mary, the declarant, is stating what she heard Louise tell her out of court. That is the potential outside hearsay. But as the Human Resources Officer, her statement, offered against the employer, is either a representative or agent admission that is being used against a party (the employer). Consequently, it is not hearsay. The inside hearsay is the statement by John to Louise. This is not hearsay because it is an admission; a statement by John, a party (Mary sued both her employer and John), used against him. So, neither statement is hearsay. Answer A is wrong because both statements are admissions and therefore are deemed not to be hearsay. Answer B is wrong because although the internal statement is an admission, so is the external statement, and so neither of these statements is hearsay. Answer C is incorrect because there is no statement against interest here. Both of these statements are party admissions.

13. Issue: Rule of completeness

The correct answer is **D**. Although Louise's recounting on cross-examination of John's out-of-court statement to her is not an admission because it is being used by and not against the party/declarant, it nevertheless is admissible on the theory that it provides better meaning and context to the admission that was admitted against him (Louise's recounting on direct examination that John had confirmed making the sexual references and touchings) and is deemed not hearsay. Answer A is incorrect because although the statement elicited on cross-examination is not an admission as it is being used by him and not against him, it nevertheless is admissible on the theory that it provides better meaning and context to the admission that was admitted against him and is deemed not hearsay. Answer B is incorrect because this statement is not an admission, as it is being used by the declarant/party and not against him. Answer C is incorrect because it is not a declaration against interest, but rather, a statement by a party.

14. Issue: State of mind exception

The correct answer is **A**. This is a classic statement that directly describes the declarant's state of mind. His statement, "I believe . . ." expressly describes the declarant's then-existing mental state and therefore falls within the Rule 803(3) exception. Answer B is incorrect because although it is a statement made by a party, it is being used by that party and not against him and so cannot constitute an admission. Answer C is incorrect because the statement falls within the state of mind exception. Answer D is incorrect because an out-of-court statement is deemed not hearsay only if it is used as circumstantial evidence of the declarant's state of mind. This statement is a direct expression of state of mind and falls within the hearsay exception of Rule 803(3) and not outside the definition of hearsay, as would be the case when a statement is used as circumstantial evidence of the declarant's state of mind and is not offered to prove the truth of the matter asserted in that statement.

15. Issue: Co-conspirator admission

The correct answer is **A**. This is an out-of-court statement. An admission by one co-conspirator can be deemed an admission by another non-declarant co-conspirator under Rule 801(d)(2)(E), but only when that statement was made in furtherance of and during the course of the conspiracy. Because the declarant referred to the completed act, the statement obviously was not made during the course of the conspiracy. It occurred after the completion of the conspiracy. Thus, it is not an admission and is an out-of-court statement offered to prove the truth of the matter asserted that does not fall within any exception and is therefore hearsay. Answer B is incorrect because as the declarant referred to the completed act, the statement obviously was not made during the course of the conspiracy. It occurred after the completion of the conspiracy. Answer C is incorrect because it is not against the declarant Tom's penal or other interest to say that someone else committed a crime. Answer D is incorrect because it is not being used to prove the police officer's state of mind. The declarant was Tom and not the police officer, and the state of mind of the police officer is irrelevant to this case.

16. Issue: Excited utterance exception

The correct answer is **C**. This is an out-of-court statement offered to prove the truth of the matter asserted therein and so is hearsay. But the fact of crying and the immediacy of the declaration indicate that the declarant Peter was in an agitated state when he made the statement concerning the agitating event. Thus, it falls within the excited utterance exception to hearsay under Rule 803(2). Answer A is incorrect because this is an excited utterance. Answer B is incorrect because the statement is not being used against the declarant/party.

Answer D is incorrect because Rule 414 admits evidence of prior acts of child molestation by the defendant and this statement only refers to the act of molestation alleged in this criminal case, not prior acts by the defendants.

17. Issue: Circumstantial use of character evidence

The correct answer is **B**. This is an example of the permissible use of prior acts to prove character for circumstantial use, i.e., to prove that the defendant acted in conformity with his character trait of molesting young children. Rule 414 is an exception to the general rule in Rule 404, i.e., the rule that does not permit evidence of character for this circumstantial purpose to be proved by evidence of prior acts. Answer A is incorrect because Rule 414 is an exception to the general rule in Rule 404 that does not permit evidence of character for this circumstantial purpose to be proved by evidence of prior acts. Answer C is incorrect because Rule 414 is predicated, in part, on the notion that evidence that the defendant engaged in prior acts of child molestation is probative of whether or not the defendant molested the child as alleged in the instant case. Answer D is incorrect because the witness Charles is testifying as to an event and not repeating what he heard in an out-of-court statement.

18. Issue: Present sense impression exception

The correct answer is **A**. The operator is repeating an out-of-court statement to prove the truth of the matter asserted, so it is a hearsay statement by the declarant. But it falls within the present sense impression of Rule 803(1) because the declarant described an event "immediately after" having observed it within the meaning of Rule 803(1). Answer B is therefore incorrect; the fact that there was a short time interval between the viewing and the recounting is not fatal to the assertion of the present sense impression exception to the hearsay rule. Answer C is incorrect because this is not character evidence; it is eyewitness testimony of an event. Answer D is incorrect because Rule 414 permits introduction of evidence of prior acts of molestation by the defendant. This declaration refers to the act of molestation alleged in the instant criminal case.

19. Issue: Statements for medical diagnosis exception

The correct answer is **A**. This is an out-of-court statement offered to prove the truth of the matter asserted but it fits within the Rule 803(4) exception for statements made for medical diagnosis. Although the statement is one of identification rather than of symptoms or causation of the symptoms, the courts routinely rule that identification of the perpetrator of violence in a child molestation case is useful to the doctor in terms of offering medical treatment and so it falls within Rule 803(4). Answer B is incorrect because although the statement is one of identification rather than of symptoms or causation of the symptoms, the courts routinely rule that identification of the perpetrator of violence in a child molestation case is useful to the doctor in terms of offering medical treatment, and so it falls within Rule 803(4). Answer C is incorrect because Rule 414 permits introduction of evidence of prior acts of molestation by the defendant. This declaration refers to the act of molestation alleged in the instant criminal case. Answer D is incorrect because Rule 413 is inapplicable to these facts; it permits evidence of prior acts of sexual assault in cases in which the defendant is charged with sexual assault. Accordingly, it does not apply to this case of child molestation.

20. Issue: Statements for medical diagnosis exception

The correct answer is **C**. This is an out-of-court statement offered to prove the truth of the matter asserted. It falls within the medical diagnosis exception because that exception also applies to statements made for the purpose of diagnosis and treatment by persons other than the patient and statements made to medical professionals other than a doctor. The cause (molestation) of the son's injury is relevant to the doctor's diagnosis and treatment (although the name of the perpetrator would not be relevant for this purpose). So, the exception applies. Answer A is incorrect because the medical diagnosis exception also applies to statements made for the purpose of diagnosis and treatment by persons other than the patient and statements made to medical professionals other than a doctor. Answer B is incorrect because the medical diagnosis exception also applies to statements made for the purpose of diagnosis and treatment by persons other than the patient and statements made to medical professionals other than a doctor. Answer D is incorrect because Rule 414 permits introduction of evidence of prior acts of molestation by the defendant. This declaration refers to the act of molestation alleged in the instant criminal case.

21. Issue: Double hearsay

The correct answer is **D**. This is a double hearsay problem. The external hearsay involves the notes. The notes constitute an out-of-court written statement, but they can be read because these facts present an example of past recollection recorded under Rule 803(5). The facts indicate that all the requirements for reading the document (a hearsay statement) are present here: it is a matter as to which the doctor once had knowledge but now cannot remember that was recorded in a document at a time when it was fresh in his mind, was accurate at the time it was made, and was made in the ordinary course of his activities. But the notes contain an internal hearsay statement — the identification of the perpetrator by Peter. That out-of-court statement is being offered to prove the truth of its contents, but it would fall within the Rule 803(4) exception for statements of medical condition because the identity of the perpetrator is relevant to psychiatric diagnosis or treatment. Thus, that part of the note can be read. Answer A is wrong because the internal hearsay statement falls within the Rule 803(4) exception and the notes can be read pursuant to the past recollection recorded doctrine of Rule 803(5). Answer B is incorrect because the elements of that doctrine are not present in this problem. Under present memory revived, the witness is shown a document, he says that it now refreshes his once-dormant memory, and then he testifies from memory. That is not the case here. Answer C is wrong because although the document is a hearsay statement, it would meet the Rule 803(4) medical diagnosis exception because the identity of the molester is relevant to the psychiatric treatment of a victim of child molestation.

22. Issue: Business records exception

The correct answer is **C**. Under Rule 803(6), records of regularly conducted activity can be admitted as an exception to the hearsay rule. There are extensive foundation requirements, but if, as stated in Answer C, they are met, then the record is admissible. Answer A is incorrect because it is insufficient. Yes, the records are hearsay, but they will be admitted under the Rule 803(6) exception if the proper foundation is laid. Answer B is incorrect because this document is clearly relevant to the defendants' alibi. Answer D is incorrect because answer C is correct.

23. Issue: Excited utterance exception

The correct answer is **B**. This is an out-of-court statement offered to prove the truth of the matter asserted, and so it is hearsay. But the declarant Peter made a statement relating to a startling event while under the stress caused by that event, and so it falls within the Rule 803(2) excited utterance exception. Answer A is incorrect because, although hearsay, it falls within an exception and so is admissible. Answer C is wrong because a defendant's Sixth Amendment Confrontation Clause rights are not violated by the admission of a hearsay statement that falls within a well recognized exception such as the excited utterance exception and the prosecution establishes that the declarant is unavailable. Because Peter, the declarant, died before trial, he obviously is unavailable. Answer D is wrong because the statement does not go to the declarant's state of mind, but is being offered to prove the truth of the matter asserted, i.e., that he was assaulted by Tom.

24. Issue: Confrontation Clause

The correct answer is **A**. The Sixth Amendment only permits the introduction of hearsay testimony falling within a well recognized exception (here, Rule 803(5)), when the prosecution establishes that the declarant is unavailable. The prosecution has not done that here. Answer B is incorrect because there is no evidence that the declarant Christopher was speaking while under the stress of the alleged advances. Answer C is wrong because although the statement is hearsay as it was made out of court to prove the truth of the matter asserted therein, it would fit under the Rule 803(4) exception for statements made for medical diagnosis or treatment. Answer D is wrong because the statement is being offered to prove the truth of the matter asserted therein and not to establish the declarant's state of mind.

25. Issue: Statements for medical diagnosis exception

The correct answer is **C**. This is an out-of-court statement offered to prove the truth of the matter asserted therein, and so is hearsay. But it was made to the doctor for the purposes of medical treatment, as the courts say that identifying the molester is relevant to psychiatric treatment; the statement also describes the nature of the touching, which is also relevant to diagnosis and treatment. So, it fits within the Rule 803(4) exception. Answer A is incorrect because although it is hearsay, it fits within the Rule 803(4) exception and is admissible. Answer B is incorrect because the declarant is a witness and is therefore subject to confrontation by the defendant, and so there is no Sixth Amendment Confrontation Clause problem. Answer D is incorrect because a witness who repeats his out-of-court statement is still offering hearsay. The question is whether or not the hearsay statement is admissible under an exception, which is available here.

26. Issue: Confrontation Clause

The correct answer is **C**. This is an out-of-court statement offered to prove the truth of the matter asserted therein, and so is hearsay. The question is whether it fits within the exception for public records in Rule 803(8) or business records in Rule 803(6). Rule 803(8) expressly excludes records created by police officers during police interrogations. Although police records could be considered a business record under Rule 803(6), the courts have ruled that Rule 803(6) cannot be applied in a way that would circumvent the policy of Rule 803(8), which is to make law enforcement reports absolutely inadmissible against defendants in criminal cases. Thus, any police report that does not qualify for admission under Rule 803(8) cannot qualify for admission under Rule 803(6). The courts do this to protect the defendant's right to confront his accusers as effectively under the business records exception, as it is under the public records exception. Admitting this hearsay statement by Christopher would deprive the defendant of his right of confrontation under the Sixth Amendment because Christopher, the declarant, is dead and now unavailable for trial. Answer A is wrong because this exception expressly does not apply to police records. Answer B is incorrect because this exception has been construed not to apply to police records. Answer D is wrong because this fact only supports exclusion, not admission, of the declarant's statement.

27. Issue: *Bruton* rule

The correct answer is **B**. This is a *Bruton* problem. First, this is an out-of-court statement offered to prove the truth of the matter asserted therein and, so is hearsay. But although it is a statement by the declarant defendant Bill, it is not considered an admission when it is offered against co-defendant, non-declarant Tom. Nevertheless, because the prejudice to Tom is too great even if the trial judge admits the testimony for the limited purpose of going only to Bill's guilt, this limiting instruction is insufficient to protect Tom, so the testimony is not admitted against either defendant. The prosecution must either try them separately or not use the statement at all. Answer A is incorrect because the limiting instruction is not sufficient to protect Tom from the prejudice that would result from the jury hearing this powerful testimony from a co-conspirator. Answer C is incorrect because it is not a co-conspirator admission because the statement was made after the completion of the conspiracy and not during the course of the conspiracy, as required under Rule 801(d)(2)(E). Answer D is incorrect because there is no double hearsay; just the recounting of Bill's hearsay declaration by the police officer.

28. Issue: *Bruton* rule

The correct answer is **C**. This is a *Bruton* problem. First, this is an out-of-court statement offered to prove the truth of the matter asserted therein and so is hearsay. It is an admission as respects the declarant defendant Bill, but it does not fall within any exception if admitted against co-defendant, non-declarant Tom. Because the prejudice to Tom is too great even if the trial judge admits the testimony for the limited purpose of going only to Bill's guilt, this limiting instruction is insufficient to protect Tom, so the testimony is not admitted against either defendant. The prosecution must either try them separately or not use the statement at all. Answer A is incorrect because under *Bruton*, the limiting instruction is not sufficient to avoid the prejudice to the non-declarant defendant. Answer B is incorrect because this statement is not a co-conspirator admission, as the statement was made after the completion of the conspiracy and not during the course of the conspiracy as required under Rule 801(d)(2)(E). Answer D is incorrect because the fact that this is a written confession as opposed to oral testimony by a police officer who heard the confession is of no consequence.

29. Issue: *Bruton* rule

The correct answer is **A**. This case falls under *Bruton*. The limited redaction here, which just eliminates the name of the non-declarant co-defendant, is not sufficient to avoid the prejudice that will accrue when the jury hears this statement against the non-declarant defendant (Tom) even with a limiting instruction. The redaction would need to eliminate all reference to both the name and existence of a co-defendant. It does not. Answer B is incorrect because the statement is not a co-conspirator admission, as the statement was made after the completion of the conspiracy and not during the course of the conspiracy as required under Rule 801(d)(2)(E). Answer C is incorrect because the limiting instruction is insufficient under *Bruton*. Answer D is incorrect because the deletion of Tom's name is not the type of redaction that eliminates the prejudice sought to be avoided under *Bruton*. It would need also to eliminate all reference in the statement to the existence of a co-defendant, which it does not.

30. Issue: Specific acts evidence of character

The correct answer is **C**. This is evidence of specific prior acts by the defendant to establish character for the purpose of proving that the defendant acted in conformity with that character trait. Under Rule 415, the evidence is admissible because this civil case seeks damages based on the defendant's commission of child molestation, and so evidence of the defendant's commission of other offenses of sexual assault, other than the one charged in this civil case, is admissible. This case was brought by Christopher and the evidence is of the defendant's molestation in the past of Peter and Anthony. Answer A is incorrect because this does not constitute evidence of habit; it is past acts going to character to show that the defendant acted consistently with that character in this case. Answer B is incorrect because although prior acts going to character are generally inadmissible under Rule 404, they are admissible in this civil case based on an allegation of child molestation under Rule 415. Answer D is incorrect because the defendant need not open the door under Rule 415 for this evidence of prior acts to be admissible.

31. Issue: Evidence of victim's character

The correct answer is **C**. This is reputation evidence going to the character of the victim offered in a civil case. Rule 415 only permits the introduction of prior acts by the defendant, and not by the victim. Rule 414 is inapplicable because it applies only to criminal cases and also only permits evidence of prior offenses of child molestation by the defendant. Answer A is incorrect because although it is hearsay, it falls within the reputation for character exception of Rule 803(21). Answer B is incorrect because Rule 415 only permits the introduction of prior acts by the defendant, and not by the victim. Rule 414 is inapplicable because it applies only to criminal cases and also only permits evidence of prior offenses of child molestation by the defendant. Answer D is incorrect because the fact that Christopher is a minor is irrelevant; although it means that this lawsuit qualifies under Rule 415 as a claim based on "child" molestation, Rule 415 does not apply because it only permits the admission of prior acts by the defendant and not the victim.

32. Issue: Evidence of character of victim

The correct answer is **B**. This is prior acts evidence going to the character of the victim offered in a civil case. Rule 415 only permits the introduction of prior acts by the defendant, and not by the victim. Rule 414 is inapplicable because it applies only to criminal cases and also only permits evidence of prior offenses of child molestation by the defendant. Rule 404(a)(2) only permits evidence of the victim's character in criminal case, and then only in the form of reputation or opinion. So, this prior acts evidence of sexual predisposition is inadmissible. Answer A is incorrect because even if it is against the declarant's penal or other interest, the declarant testified and so is not available, and the Rule 804(b)(3) exception to the hearsay can only be used when the declarant, here Lou, is unavailable. Answer C is incorrect because the evidence does not fall within Rules 414, 415 or 404. Rule 415 only permits the introduction of prior acts by the defendant and not by the victim. Rule 414 is inapplicable because it applies only to criminal cases and also only permits evidence of prior offenses of child molestation by the defendant. Rule 404(a)(2) only permits evidence of the victim's character in criminal case, and then only in the form of reputation or opinion. So, this prior acts evidence of sexual predisposition is inadmissible. Answer D is incorrect because this is an irrelevant fact in this context.

33. Issue: Confrontation Clause

The correct answer is **D**. The defendant was charged with committing a bank robbery in Los Angeles. He wants to offer evidence that establishes an alibi that he was in San Francisco at the time he is alleged to have robbed the bank in Los Angeles. This evidence is hearsay and does not fall within any express exception. But to preclude the defendant from offering this evidence that is crucial to his defense, particularly when the declarant is now unavailable because he is dead, would violate his Sixth amendment right under the Confrontation Clause. Answer A is incorrect because the courts apply Rule 803(6) consistently with Rule 803(8), i.e., they do not admit any police report under Rule 803(6) that would be inadmissible under Rule 803(8). Answer B is incorrect because the statement does not fall within the Rule 803(8) public records exception, which expressly excludes police reports. Answer C is wrong because the declarant police officer was not excited and was not speaking about the exciting event when he made the out-of-court statement.

34. Issue: Definition of hearsay

The correct answer is **A**. This is an out-of-court statement offered to prove the truth of the matter asserted therein, and so it is hearsay and does not fall within any exception mentioned in these answers. Answer B is incorrect because this statement does not fall under Rule 801(d)(1), as it is not a prior statement by a witness because the declarant teller is not a witness. Answer C is incorrect because to fit within the former testimony exception of Rule 804(b)(1), that former testimony must have been subject to cross-examination by the same party against whom it is now offered, as it is being offered now in a criminal case. The defendant had no opportunity to cross-examine the declarant before the grand jury. Answer D is incorrect because this fact is irrelevant. The key issue for prior statement purposes under Rule 801(d)(1) is whether the declarant is a witness and the teller was not a witness. It does not matter why he was not a witness.

35. Issue: Unavailability for hearsay purposes

The correct answer is **B**. The grand jury testimony is hearsay. By invoking his Fifth Amendment right against self-incrimination, the defendant has made himself unavailable. A party who makes himself unavailable cannot take advantage of that to assert a hearsay exception that requires unavailability. Consequently, he cannot take advantage of the former testimony exception under Rule 804(d)(1). No other exception applies. Answer A is incorrect because the former testimony exception of Rule 804(d)(1) applies only when the declarant is unavailable; here, the defendant made himself unavailable and so cannot take advantage of that rule. Answer C is incorrect because the statement is being offered by the declarant party and is not being offered against him. Answer D is incorrect because a prior statement must be one made by a witness and by taking the Fifth, the defendant chose not to be a witness.

36. Issue: Definition of hearsay

The correct answer is **C**. This is an out-of-court statement offered to prove the truth of the matter asserted therein and so is hearsay that does not fit within any exception mentioned here. The dying declaration exception does not apply because that exception applies only to statements made concerning the cause of what the declarant believed to be his impending death. The declarant was under a belief of impending death, but from cancer; his statement is about a bank robbery and not his cancer. Answer A is incorrect because the dying declaration exception does not apply; that exception applies only to statements made concerning the cause of what the declarant believed to be his impending death. The declarant was under a belief of impending death, but from cancer; his statement is about a bank robbery and not his cancer. Answer B is incorrect because the availability of the wife is irrelevant. The key issue in hearsay is the unavailability of the declarant and therefore the inability to cross-examine the declarant. Answer D is incorrect because the evidence is offered to prove that Jones committed the robbery, not to establish the declarant's state of mind.

37. Issue: Former testimony exception and unavailability

The correct answer is **D**. This is an out-of-court statement offered to prove the truth of the matter asserted therein, and so is hearsay. The only possible exception here is the former testimony exception of Rule 804(b)(1), but that requires that the declarant be unavailable and that fact must be established by the party asserting the exception. That showing was not made here. Answer A is wrong because to fit within the former testimony exception of Rule 804(b)(1), the declarant, the vice president, must be unavailable. There is no evidence of that here and that must be established by the party asserting the exception. Answer B is incorrect because a prior statement must be a statement made by a witness in this case, and the vice president has not been called as a witness in the civil case. Answer C is incorrect because although the insurance company was not a party to the criminal prosecution, the evidence could come in under Rule 804(b)(1) if the declarant had been unavailable and the prosecution in the criminal case had the same opportunity and motive to cross-examine this testimony, as the insurance company would have in the civil case. So, the fact that the insurance company was not a party to the criminal case is not fatal in and of itself.

38. Issue: Former testimony exception

The correct answer is **D**. This is an out-of-court statement offered to prove the truth of the matter asserted therein, and so is hearsay. The only possible exception here is the former testimony exception of Rule 804(b)(1), which requires unavailability of the declarant. The declarant is dead, and so is unavailable. But Rule 804(d)(1) also requires that if the former testimony is being asserted in a civil case, the opponent of that evidence in the former hearing must have had the same opportunity and motive to cross-examine it as the opponent in the civil case, here, the insurance company, would have. If, as assumed in answer D, that shared motive and opportunity is not present, then the exception does not apply. Answer A is incorrect because Rule 804(d)(1) not only requires that the declarant be unavailable, it also requires that if the former testimony is being asserted in a civil case, the opponent of that evidence in the former hearing must have had the same opportunity and motive to cross-examine it as the opponent in the civil case, here, the insurance company, would have. So the answer in A is insufficient. Answer B is incorrect because a prior statement must be made by a witness to the instant case, and the vice president was not a witness. Answer C is incorrect because although the insurance company was not a party to the criminal prosecution, the evidence could come in under Rule 804(b)(1) if the declarant is unavailable and the prosecution in the criminal case had the same opportunity and motive to cross-examine this testimony as the insurance company would have in the civil case. So, the fact that the insurance company was not a party to the criminal case is not fatal in and of itself.

39. Issue: Dying declaration

The correct answer is **B**. This is an out-of-court statement offered to prove the truth of the matter asserted therein, and so is hearsay that does not fit within any exception mentioned here. Answer "A" is incorrect because the dying declaration exception does not apply; that exception applies only to statements made concerning the cause of what the declarant believed to be his impending death. The declarant was under a belief of impending death, but of death from cancer. His statement is about the videotaping issue and not his cancer. Answer C is incorrect because the dying declaration exception of Rule 804(b)(2) is available both in homicide and civil cases, and this is a civil case. So, the fact that this is not a homicide case is not why the dying declaration exception cannot be used here. Answer D is incorrect because the statement is offered to prove the truth of the matter asserted and not the declarant's state of mind.

40. Issue: Business records exception

The correct answer is **C**. Ordinarily, police reports cannot be admitted as business records. They are inadmissible under Rule 803(8) (public records) because that hearsay exception contains an express exclusion for police reports. Generally the courts construe Rule 803(6) consistently with Rule 803(8) so that police reports that cannot come in as public records cannot be admitted as business records. But an exception to this doctrine is acknowledged when the author of the report testifies. Under those circumstances, the defendant's Sixth Amendment right of confrontation is satisfied because the defendant can cross-examine the note-taker at trial. It is true that the defendant could not cross-examine the note-taker when the notes were taken, but this post facto cross-examination opportunity is deemed sufficient for Sixth Amendment purposes. Thus, the records are admissible as business records under Rule 803(6). Answer A is wrong because this evidence is deemed to fall within the business records exception. Answer B is wrong because the public records exception does not apply to police records. Answer D is incorrect because the fact that a hearsay declarant testifies at trial does not make his out-of-court statement not hearsay. It is still hearsay; the question then becomes whether or not it falls within an exception.

41. Issue: Dying declaration

The correct answer is **C**. This is an out-of-court statement offered to prove the truth of the matter asserted therein and so is hearsay. Is it a dying declaration? Well, it was made under belief of impending death and does concern the cause of his impending death. But the rule requires the statement to be a product of the declarant's personal knowledge and the reference to the Surgeon General's report reflects the government's knowledge, not the declarant's knowledge. Answer A is incorrect because dying declarations are admissible in civil cases as well as in homicide cases. They are only unavailable in non-homicide criminal cases. Answer B is incorrect because this does not fulfill the requirement that a dying declaration be the product of the declarant's personal knowledge and the reference to the Surgeon General's report reflects the government's knowledge, not the declarant's knowledge. Answer D is incorrect because this statement is offered to prove the truth of the matter asserted therein and not the declarant's state of mind.

42. Issue: Dying declaration

The correct answer is **A**. This is an out-of-court statement offered to prove the truth of the matter asserted therein and so is hearsay and does not fit within any exception. Answer B is incorrect because a dying declaration can only be admitted in a criminal case for homicide and this is a bank robbery, i.e., non-homicide case. The statement also does not go to the cause of the declarant's impending death. Answer C is incorrect because it is not made under circumstances in which a reasonable declarant would anticipate that the statement was against his or her penal interest and therefore would not lie. Under these circumstances, the declarant believed that he was dying and therefore was effectively immune from criminal prosecution. Consequently, it was not a statement against his penal interest. Answer D is incorrect because an admission must be offered against the declarant party and this was not a statement made by a party to the case, but by the teller.

43. Issue: Declaration against interest

The correct answer is **A**. This is an out-of-court statement offered to prove the truth of the matter asserted therein and so is hearsay. To fit within the declaration against penal interest exception of Rule 804(3), the declarant must be unavailable (which he is, because he is now dead). But where the out-of-court statement that exposes the declarant to criminal liability is offered to exculpate the defendant, that statement is not admissible unless corroborating circumstances indicate its trustworthiness. Because the defense offered no other evidence, there is no evidence of such corroborating circumstances, and so the evidence is inadmissible as uncorroborated. Answer B is incorrect because to fit within the declaration against penal interest exception of Rule 804(3), the declarant must not only be unavailable (he is because he is now dead), but if the statement that would expose the declarant to criminal liability is offered to exculpate the defendant, it is not admissible unless corroborating circumstances indicate its trustworthiness. Because the defense offered no other evidence, there is no evidence of such corroborating circumstances. Answer C is incorrect because it is not a statement by a party offered against that party. The declarant was Charles, who is not a party to this case. Answer D is incorrect because the statement is not against the interest of the witness, Wilbur. Moreover, Wilbur was not the out-of-court declarant.

44. Issue: Character directly in issue

The correct answer is **C**. Rule 404(a) generally precludes the use of character evidence for circumstantial purposes, i.e., to prove that the individual acted consistently with that character trait. It does not, however, preclude the use of character evidence when character is directly in issue. Here, the defense in the civil case maintains that the reason for its action is that Sally is untrustworthy. Consequently, her character for that trait is directly in issue and the plaintiff can offer evidence of it in any form, i.e., reputation, opinion, or prior acts. Answer A is incorrect because this is opinion testimony from the witness who is not relating an out-of-court statement. Answer B is incorrect because the plaintiff's character is directly in issue. Answer D is incorrect because this is opinion, not reputation evidence.

45. Issue: Character directly in issue

The correct answer is **A**. Rule 404(a) generally precludes the use of character evidence for circumstantial purposes, i.e., to prove that the individual acted consistently with that character trait. It does not, however, preclude the use of character evidence when character is directly in issue. Here, the defense in the civil case maintains that the reason for its action is that Sally is untrustworthy. Consequently, her character for that trait is directly in issue and the plaintiff can offer evidence of it in any form, i.e., reputation, opinion, or prior acts. So, the fact that this evidence is evidence of prior acts is not a problem. Answer B is incorrect because the plaintiff's character is directly in issue. Answer C is incorrect because this is not hearsay testimony; the reference to out-of-court statements is not being used to prove the truth of the statements Lynn made to Sally, but the fact that Sally never revealed the contents to anyone else. Answer D is incorrect because answer A is correct.

46. Issue: Specific acts evidence of character

The correct answer is **A**. The issue is whether or not the evidence of the prior acts of harassment by the plaintiff's supervisor is permissible or impermissible character evidence. That turns on whether character is directly in issue or is being used circumstantially to prove action in conformity with that trait. The character of the supervisor is not an issue in this case. The issue is the company's knowledge of what he was doing and whether he harassed Sally. Consequently, this is an attempt to make circumstantial use of character evidence, which is prohibited in civil cases by Rule 404(a). Answer B is incorrect because this is not hearsay, as the witness is not testifying as to any out-of-court statement. Answer C is incorrect because Rule 404(a) prohibits the use of evidence of the character of a non-witness in civil case to prove action in conformity with that character trait. Answer D is incorrect because the witness is testifying from her own memory and not repeating any out-of-court statement. Thus, whether or not the statement constitutes a non-hearsay admission is not relevant here.

47. Issue: Circumstantial use of character evidence

The correct answer is **C**. Rule 404(a) precludes the circumstantial use of character evidence of a non-witness in civil cases to establish action in conformity with that character trait, regardless of whether it is offered in the form of reputation, opinion, or specific acts. Answer A is incorrect because this reputation evidence fits within the Rule 803(21) exception for reputation of character. So, it is not excluded by Rule 802. Answer B is incorrect because the fact that the evidence is not barred by the hearsay rule does not mean that it is not precluded by some other rule, such as 404(a). Answer D is incorrect because Rule 404(a) precludes the circumstantial use of character evidence concerning a non-witness in civil cases to establish action in conformity with that character trait, regardless of which party offers it and whether it is offered in the form of reputation, opinion or specific acts.

48. Issue: Evidence of defendant's character

The correct answer is **A**. Rule 404(a) generally prohibits the introduction of character evidence for circumstantial purposes, i.e., to prove action in conformity with that character trait. Although Rule 404(a)(1) allows reputation and opinion evidence of a criminal defendant's character, the prosecution can only offer evidence of the defendant's character after the defendant has put his character in issue by offering admissible evidence of his good character. The defendant did not open the door in this case, so the prosecution can not offer evidence of the defendant's character. Answer B is incorrect because the defendant did not open the door to such evidence per Rule 404(a)(1). Answer C is incorrect because reputation for character testimony falls within the Rule 803(21) exception to the hearsay rule. Answer D is incorrect because although the evidence is not excluded under the hearsay rule, it is excluded under Rule 404(a).

49. Issue: Evidence of defendant's character

The correct answer is **B**. Rule 404(a) generally prohibits the introduction of character evidence for circumstantial purposes, i.e., to prove action in conformity with that character trait. But Rule 404(a)(1) allows reputation and opinion evidence of a criminal defendant's character to be offered by the defendant. That is what has happened here, because this is reputation evidence in a criminal case offered by the defendant to establish his good character. Answer A is wrong because this is admissible under Rule 404(a)(1), as it is reputation evidence offered by the defendant to establish his good character. Answer C is wrong because this reputation for character testimony fits within the Rule 803(21) hearsay exception. Answer D is wrong because answer B is correct.

50. Issue: Specific acts evidence of character

The correct answer is **C**. Rule 404(a) generally prohibits the introduction of character evidence for circumstantial purposes, i.e., to prove action in conformity with that character trait. Rule 404(a)(1) allows reputation and opinion evidence of a criminal defendant's character to be offered by the defendant; however, it permits only reputation or opinion testimony, and this is evidence of prior specific acts and so is precluded by Rule 404(b). Answer A is incorrect because this use of specific acts evidence of the defendant's character is prohibited by Rule 404(b). Answer B is incorrect because the defendant's character is not directly in issue; this evidence is coming in for circumstantial purposes, i.e., to prove action in conformity with the defendant's good character. Answer D is incorrect because this factor is irrelevant. It is prohibited character evidence under Rule 404(b).

51. Issue: Specific acts evidence of character

The correct answer is **A**. Under Rule 404(a)(1), once the defendant opens the door to her good character, which she did here, the prosecution can offer evidence of her bad character. But that evidence must take the form of opinion or reputation when offered by the prosecution's character witness, as opposed to the prosecution's cross-examination of the defendant's character witness. Because the neighbor was the prosecution's witness, she can only testify in the form of reputation or opinion; this is evidence of prior specific acts, so it is excluded under Rule 404(b). Answer B is incorrect because although the defendant opened the door, the prosecution can only reply with opinion or reputation evidence when not cross-examining the defendant's character witness but offering its own character witness to testify against the defendant. Answer C is incorrect because the evidence would be relevant to character if in the proper form. Answer D is incorrect because answer A is correct.

52. Issue: Specific acts evidence of character

The correct answer is **B**. Rule 404(b) precludes the use of specific acts evidence to establish the defendant's character when it is offered to prove that the defendant acted consistently with that character trait in the instant criminal case. But where that specific acts evidence is not offered to prove character, but something else, such as the defendant's intent, then it is not prohibited under

Rule 404(b). The defendant has put her intent in issue and that is what this evidence goes to prove and so it is admissible under Rule 404(b). Answer A is incorrect because although Rule 404(b) precludes the use of specific acts evidence to establish the defendant's character when it is offered to prove that the defendant acted consistently with that character trait in the instant criminal case, where that specific acts evidence is not offered to prove character but something else, such as the defendant's intent, then it is not prohibited under Rule 404(b). The defendant has put her intent in issue and that is what this evidence goes to prove, and so it is admissible under Rule 404(b). Answer C is incorrect because this evidence is not going to prove the defendant's bad character, but her intent, and so the rule in 404(a)(1) does not apply concerning the need for the defendant to open the door to evidence of her character when used to prove action in conformity with the character trait. Answer D is incorrect because answer B is correct.

53. Issue: Evidence of victim's character

The correct answer is **C**. Under Rule 404(a)(2) a criminal defendant can offer evidence of the victim's pertinent character trait. Because this is a self-defense case, the victim's violent character is relevant. Such evidence must take the form of reputation or opinion and this is reputation evidence, so it is admissible under Rule 404(a)(2). Answer A is incorrect because this reputation for character evidence fits within the Rule 803(21) exception to the hearsay rule. Answer B is incorrect because under Rule 404(a)(2) a criminal defendant can offer evidence of the victim's pertinent character trait. Because this is a self-defense case, the victim's violent character is relevant. Such evidence must take the form of reputation or opinion and this is reputation evidence, so it is admissible under Rule 404(a)(2). Answer D is incorrect because answer C is correct.

54. Issue: Evidence of defendant's character

The correct answer is **D**. Under Rule 404(a)(1), once the criminal defendant has opened the door by offering evidence of the victim's character through appropriate reputation or opinion evidence (which occurred here), the prosecution then can respond with reputation or opinion evidence concerning that same character trait in the defendant. Because the defense opened the door with evidence of the victim's violent character, the prosecution can respond with reputation or opinion evidence of the defendant's violent character. This is opinion evidence, so it is admissible. Answer A is wrong because under Rule 404(a)(1) once the defendant puts the victim's character in issue, the prosecution can offer evidence of the defendant's character with respect to the trait of victim character that was offered by the defense. The defense does not have to put the defendant's character in issue for the prosecution to be able to offer this evidence. Answer B is incorrect because this is not hearsay, but opinion testimony by the witness. Answer C is incorrect because this is proper character evidence under Rule 404(a)(1).

55. Issue: Cross-examination of character witness

The correct answer is **C**. This is specific acts evidence of character, which is generally prohibited by Rule 404(a) when used to prove character and action conformity therewith. Under Rule 405(a), a character witness's credibility as a character witness can be challenged on cross-examination by inquiring into the depth of the character witness' knowledge of the person about whose character he or she is testifying. On direct examination, Sam offered reputation evidence of the victim Stan's character for violence. This is permitted under Rule 404(a)(2) because it came in the form of reputation evidence. Under Rule 405(a), on cross-examination of that victim character witness, the witness can be asked about "relevant" specific instances of conduct by the person as to whose character (the victim) he testified. Here, however, the cross-examination of character witness Sam inquired into specific acts of lying by victim Stan when Sam had testified only about Stan's violent character. Consequently, this is not evidence of "relevant" prior acts because it goes to a character trait of the victim, truthfulness, which was not discussed by the character witness on direct examination. Rules 608 and 609 dealing with impeaching a witness with prior acts, even convictions, going to truthfulness are not applicable here because the evidence here is going to the character of the victim, Stan, who was not a witness. Answer A is incorrect because the witness is being asked whether he heard those out-of-court statements and not whether or not they are true. In other words, this is an out-of-court statement or statements offered for the purpose of impeachment and not to prove the truth of the matter asserted. Consequently, it is not hearsay. Answer B is incorrect because Rule 405(a) only permits inquiry into "relevant" specific acts on cross-examination of a character witness; here, the character witness testified as to the victim's violent character and is being asked on cross-examination about the victim's prior acts relating to truthfulness. Consequently, this does not constitute inquiry into "relevant" prior acts under Rule 405(a). Answer D is incorrect because the evidence is offered to impeach the credibility of the character witness and not to establish his state of mind.

56. Issue: Specific acts evidence of character

The correct answer is **C**. The defendant offered reputation evidence of the victim's character. The prosecution can, under Rule 404(a)(1) offer evidence of that same character trait of the defendant, but it must be the same character trait and it must be in the form of opinion or reputation evidence. Here the prosecution is offering specific acts evidence, which is prohibited by Rule 404(b). Although it goes to the same character trait of violence that the defendant put in play with respect to the victim, it is in the prohibited form of specific acts rather than opinion or reputation, so it is prohibited by Rule 404(b). Answer A is incorrect because this is not hearsay testimony. Answer B is incorrect because Rule 404(b) prohibits the use of specific acts evidence to challenge the defendant's character on direct examination of a character witness. Answer D is incorrect because the evidence is being offered to prove the defendant's character and not the witness's state of mind.

57. Issue: Cross-examination of character witness

The correct answer is **A**. Rule 405(b) permits the opponent of a character witness to challenge the credibility of that character witness on cross-examination by delving into the basis of support for the reputation or opinion testimony offered by the character witness. That can be done by asking questions that refer to prior specific acts by the person whose character the character witness has testified about. Because this character witness offered reputation evidence, it can be challenged by asking if the witness had "heard" about contradictory specific acts by the person about whose character the witness testified. Answer B is incorrect because Rule 405(b) permits the opponent of a character witness to challenge the credibility of that character witness on cross-examination by delving into the basis of support for the reputation or opinion testimony offered by the character witness. That can be done by asking questions that refer to prior specific acts by the person about whose character the character witness has testified. Because this character witness offered reputation evidence, it can be challenged by asking if the witness had "heard" about contradictory specific acts by the person about whose character the witness testified. Answer C is incorrect because it is within the proper scope of cross-examination of a character witness when the criminal defendant was permitted under Rule 404(a)(2) to offer reputation testimony as to the victim's pertinent character trait. Answer D is incorrect because answer A is correct.

58. Issue: Evidence of victim's character

The correct answer is **C**. Under Rule 404(a)(2), when the defendant offers evidence that the alleged victim was the first aggressor, as is the case here, the prosecution can respond with opinion or reputation evidence of the victim's character for peacefulness if it is in a homicide case. This is a homicide case. The witness offered reputation evidence and so it is admissible under Rule 404(a)(2). Answer A is incorrect because this reputation for character testimony fits within the Rule 803(21) hearsay exception. Answer B is incorrect because under Rule 404(a)(2), when the defendant offers evidence that the alleged victim was the first aggressor, as is the case here, the prosecution can respond with opinion or reputation evidence of the victim's character for peacefulness if it is in a homicide case. This is a homicide case. The witness offered reputation evidence and so it is admissible under Rule 404(a)(2). Answer D is incorrect because answer C is correct.

59. Issue: Evidence of victim's character

The correct answer is **A**. Under Rule 404(a)(2), when the defendant offers evidence that the alleged victim was the first aggressor, the prosecution can respond with opinion or reputation evidence of the victim's character for peacefulness if it is in a homicide case. Here the prosecutor is offering specific acts, rather than opinion or reputation evidence of the victim's character for peacefulness, and that is not permitted under Rule 404(a)(2) and is prohibited by Rule 404(b). Answer B is incorrect because this evidence of the victim's character came in the impermissible form of specific acts and not via reputation or opinion, which would have been permitted since the defendant did offer evidence that the victim was the initial aggressor. Answer C is incorrect because this is character evidence offered to prove that the victim acted consistently with his peaceable character in this case. Answer D is incorrect because the fact that it does not relate to the defendant's character is irrelevant. The prosecution under Rule 404(a)(2) can offer evidence of the victim's character for peacefulness if the defense offers evidence that the victim was the initial aggressor.

60. Issue: Habit

The correct answer is **B**. Rule 406 permits evidence of habit in either a civil or criminal case to prove that the person involved acted consistently with that habit in the instant case. Habit must be a consistent response to a regularly occurring situation. That is the case here. Consequently, the evidence is admissible under Rule 406. Answer A is incorrect because this is habit evidence; it is not character evidence. Answer C is incorrect because the witness is not testifying that he heard an out-of-court statement. It is not hearsay. Answer D is incorrect because this is not character evidence; it is evidence of habit.

61. Issue: Specific acts to prove other than character

The correct answer is **A**. Although this is evidence of prior acts, if it is offered to prove something other than the defendant's character, it is admissible under Rule 404(b). With the proper foundation, this evidence could be shown to be probative of the defendant's preparation or plan for the murder by, for example, showing that the guns that were stolen were the ones used in the murder of Stan. Answer B is incorrect because this evidence was not offered to prove character but to prove preparation or plan under Rule 404(b). With the proper foundation, this evidence could be shown to be probative of the defendant's preparation or plan for the murder by, for example, showing that the guns that were stolen were the ones used in the murder of Stan. Answer C is incorrect because this prior acts evidence is not being used to establish character and action by the defendant consistent with that character trait. If it were offered for that purpose, it would be inadmissible under Rule 404(b). Answer D is wrong because this is irrelevant; the evidence is not offered by the prosecution to establish the defendant's character to prove that he acted consistently with that character trait. On the other hand, if that were its purpose, then it would be excluded under Rule 404(a)(1) because the defendant had not opened the door.

62. Issue: Victim's prior sexual history or predisposition

The correct answer is **A**. This is evidence of prior sexual acts by the victim in a sexual assault case. Under Rule 412(b)(1)(A), evidence of the victim's prior sexual history or sexual predisposition is inadmissible in a criminal case when the evidence concerns the victim's prior sexual history with persons other than the defendant unless the evidence is offered to prove that the source of physical evidence, such as semen, was someone other than the defendant. That is not the purpose here. The defense is offering this to prove consent. The evidence is inadmissible. Answer B is wrong because under Rule 412(b)(1)(A), evidence of the victim's prior sexual history or sexual predisposition is inadmissible in a criminal case when the evidence concerns the victim's prior sexual history with persons other than the defendant unless the evidence is offered to prove that the source of physical evidence, such as semen, was someone other than the defendant. That is not the purpose here. Answer C is incorrect because this is not hearsay; the witnesses would testify as to their conduct, not what they heard in an out-of-court conversation. Answer D is incorrect because answer A is correct.

63. Issue: Victim's prior sexual history or predisposition

The correct answer is **B**. Under Rule 412(b)(1)(B), evidence of the prior sexual history between an alleged victim of a sexual assault and the defendant is admissible if offered to prove consent. That is the purpose here, and so this evidence is admissible and not precluded by the general rule against offering evidence of a sexual assault victim's prior sexual history found in Rule 412(a). Answer A is incorrect because the evidence is admissible under Rule 412(b)(1)(B) where, as here, evidence of the prior sexual history between an alleged victim of a sexual assault and the defendant is offered to prove consent. Answer C is incorrect because this is not habit evidence. Answer D is incorrect because this evidence is deemed relevant under Rule 412(b)(1)(B).

64. Issue: Victim's prior sexual history or predisposition

The correct answer is **C**. Under Rule 412(a), evidence of the sexual history or sexual predisposition of an alleged victim of a sexual assault is inadmissible subject only to the exceptions contained in Rule 412(b), none of which apply to this case. Answer A is wrong because under Rule 412(a), evidence of the sexual history or sexual predisposition of an alleged victim of a sexual assault is inadmissible subject only to the exceptions contained in Rule 412(b), none of which apply to this case. Answer B is incorrect because this reputation for character evidence falls within the Rule 803(21) hearsay exception. Answer D is incorrect because the fact that Loraine is the victim does not by itself preclude evidence of her sexual history. Evidence of it could come in if it fell within any of the three exceptions found in Rule 412(b).

65. Issue: Victim's prior sexual history or predisposition

The correct answer is **C**. Under Rule 412(a), evidence of the sexual history or sexual predisposition of an alleged victim of a sexual assault is inadmissible subject only to the exceptions contained in Rule 412(b), none of which apply to this case. The fact that this evidence is in the form of opinion makes no difference. No type of evidence of the victim's sexual past, regardless of whether it is opinion, reputation, or past acts, is admissible unless it fits within one of the three exceptions in Rule 412(b). So, the fact that this is opinion evidence as opposed to the reputation evidence in Question 64 does not call for a different answer. Answer A is wrong because under Rule 412(a), evidence of the sexual history or sexual predisposition of an alleged victim of a sexual assault is inadmissible subject only to the exceptions contained in 412(b), none of which apply to this case. No type of evidence of the victim's sexual past, regardless of whether it is opinion, reputation, or past acts, is admissible unless it fits within one of the three exceptions in Rule 412(b). Answer B is incorrect because this reputation for character evidence falls within the Rule 803(21) hearsay exception. Answer D is incorrect because the fact that Loraine is the victim does not by itself preclude evidence of her sexual history. Evidence of it could come in if it fell within any of the three exceptions found in Rule 412(b).

66. Issue: Defendant's prior acts in sexual assault case

The correct answer is **B**. Rule 413(a) creates an exception to the general rule of 404(b) that even after the defendant has opened the door by offering admissible (opinion or reputation) evidence of his good character, evidence of a defendant's bad character, when used to prove action in conformity therewith, cannot be offered through another character witness who testifies as to specific acts (as opposed to reputation or opinion). Under Rule 413, evidence of prior, unrelated acts of sexual assault allegedly committed by the defendant charged with a separate sexual assault is admissible to show that the defendant acted consistently with that character trait. Answer A is incorrect because the evidence is admissible under Rule 413(a). Rule 413(a) creates an exception to the general rule of Rule 404(b), which provides that even after the defendant has opened the door by placing his character in issue, evidence of a defendant's bad character, when used to prove action in conformity therewith, cannot be admitted into evidence in the form of specific acts. Under Rule 413(a), evidence of prior, unrelated acts of sexual assault allegedly committed by the defendant charged with a separate sexual assault is admissible to show that the defendant acted consistently with that character trait. Answer C is incorrect because Rule 413(a) does not require the prosecution to wait until the defendant has opened the door. This is an exception to the general rule in 404(a)(1) that does require the prosecution in criminal cases not involving sexual assault, to wait until the defendant has opened the door before challenging the bad character of the defendant. Answer D is incorrect because this is not hearsay testimony. The witnesses are testifying as to what happened to them and not as to what they heard in an out-of-court conversation.

67. Issue: Defendant's prior acts in sexual assault case

The correct answer is **A**. Rule 413(a) only permits evidence of prior acts of sexual assault to come in against a defendant in a sexual assault case. This is evidence of prior acts of robbery. Thus, the applicable Rule is 404(a)(1) and that does not permit evidence of the defendant's character to be offered by the prosecution until the defendant has opened the door, and then only in the form of reputation or opinion, not specific acts. Answer B is incorrect because it is not sufficient that Lance is charged with sexual assault for Rule 413(a) to come into play. Rule 413(a) only permits evidence of prior acts of sexual assault, and this is evidence of prior robberies. Answer C is incorrect because Rule 413(a) is not limited to prior convictions. It permits evidence of any alleged acts of sexual assault, charged or non-charged. Answer D is incorrect because answer A is correct.

68. Issue: Victim's prior acts in sexual assault case

The correct answer is **A**. Under Rule 412(b)(1)(B), evidence of an alleged sexual assault victim's prior sexual history with the defendant is only admissible to prove consent. Here the defendant is not raising that defense, and so the evidence is barred by Rule 412(a), which does not generally allow evidence of a sexual assault victim's prior sexual history to be admitted. Answer B is incorrect because the defendant did not assert the defense of consent and so the evidence is not permitted under Rule 412(b)(1)(B). Under Rule 412(b)(1)(B), evidence of an alleged sexual assault victim's prior sexual history with the defendant is only admissible to prove consent. Here the defendant is not raising that defense, and so the evidence is barred by Rule 412(a), which does not generally allow evidence of a sexual assault victim's prior sexual history to be admitted. Answer C is incorrect because this is not hearsay testimony. The witness is testifying as to an event that occurred and not what he heard someone say in an out-of-court conversation. Answer D is incorrect because this is not hearsay testimony. The witness is testifying as to an event that occurred and not what he heard someone say in an out-of-court conversation

69. Issue: Victim's prior acts in sexual assault case

The correct answer is **D**. This evidence of the alleged victim's prior sexual history would generally be excluded by Rule 412(a). It also does not fit within the exceptions codified at Rule 412(b)(1)(A) or (B) because it does not involve evidence of sexual activity between the victim and the defendant — (b)(1)(B) — or between the victim and someone else — (b)(1)(A) — to prove that the source of the physical evidence was someone other than the defendant. Because the victim testified that Lance sexually assaulted her, however, Lance is entitled to establish that she has a motive to lie. If he is denied that opportunity by not being able to offer the testimony of Virginia, which would establish a motive for the victim to lie (because she did not want her lover to know that she had sex with someone else), then the defendant is being denied his constitutional right to present an adequate defense. Consequently, this testimony fits within the exception codified at 412(b)(1)(C). Answer A is incorrect because this evidence of prior sexual acts is permitted under Rule 412(b)(1)(C). Answer B is incorrect because the fact that it does not fall within the exception of 412(b)(1)(A) does not mean that it is not within the exception of 412(b)(1)(C). Answer C is incorrect because Rule 412 presumes that this evidence is relevant.

70. Issue: Victim's prior acts in sexual assault case

The correct answer is **B**. Rule 412(b)(1)(A) permits evidence of an alleged sexual assault victim's prior sexual acts with someone other than the defendant, but only when that evidence is offered to prove that the source of the physical evidence, such as semen, is someone other than the defendant. This evidence is being offered for that purpose because Lance is alleging that the victim was assaulted and beaten by someone else. Consequently, it is admissible under Rule 412(b)(1)(A). Answer A is wrong because the evidence is admissible under Rule 412(b)(1)(A). Rule 412(b)(1)(A) permits evidence of an alleged sexual assault victim's prior sexual acts with someone other than the defendant, but only when that evidence is offered to prove that the source of the physical evidence, such as semen, is someone other than the defendant. This evidence is being offered for that purpose because Lance is alleging that the victim was assaulted and beaten by someone else. Answer C is incorrect because although this is specific acts evidence and would be excluded as evidence of the victim's character under Rule 404 in any non-sexual assault case, this is a sexual assault case, and so the relevant rule is 412 and not 404 and it is admissible under Rule 412(b)(1)(A). Answer D is incorrect because this evidence is not being offered to establish the defendant's state of mind but to prove that someone else was the source of the injury suffered by the victim.

71. Issue: Agent admission

The correct answer is **D**. This testimony clearly falls within the classic definition of hearsay in that the witnesses is repeating what she heard someone else say out of court to prove the truth of the matter asserted, that the odors were bad and that they informed the company about it. Under Rule 801(d)(2)(d), it is an agent admission. These were supervisory employees discussing a matter within the scope of their employment as supervisors. Answer B is wrong because the statement is not against the supervisors' pecuniary or other interests. Moreover, even if it were, declarations against interest are hearsay and they only fall within an exception. This answer states that, like admissions, they are not hearsay. That is incorrect. Answer C is incorrect because an admission is defined to be not hearsay; it is not deemed hearsay but within an exception.

72. Issue: Subsequent remedial measures

The correct answer is **A**. This is classic evidence of subsequent remedial measures to establish culpability. Answer B is incorrect because the witness is repeating out-of-court statements by the supervisors and these statements do not constitute agent admissions because the statements do not relate to matters within the scope of their employment. But even if the statements were deemed to be admissions, and not hearsay, this answer is not correct because the fact that evidence is not barred by the hearsay rule does not guarantee its admissibility; it can be excluded by some other rule such as, in this case, Rule 407. Answer C is incorrect because even if it went to prove control or feasibility, that would not be sufficient under Rule 407. The Rule only allows admission of evidence of subsequent remedial action to prove control or feasibility after that issue has been controverted. There is no suggestion that the defendant had raised either of those issues. Answer D is incorrect because answers B and C are incorrect.

73. Issue: Compromise negotiations

The correct answer is **C**. Rule 408 excludes evidence of compromise negotiation offers only when part of an attempt to compromise a claim that was disputed as to either its validity or amount. The rule does not apply when both the validity and amount of the claim are not in dispute. While it is true that the amount of this claim is not in dispute, the validity of the claim remains in dispute. Consequently, Rule 408 does apply and precludes admission. Answer A is incorrect because although the statement is technically hearsay, under Rule 801(d)(2)(C) it is deemed not hearsay as an admission because it is an out-of-court statement by a party (the plaintiff) offered against that party. Answer B is wrong because it refers to an admission as an exception to the hearsay rule and an admission is defined as not being hearsay at all. Answer D is incorrect because Rule 408 excludes evidence of compromise negotiation offers only when part of an attempt to compromise a claim that was disputed as to either its validity or amount. The rule does not apply when both the validity and amount of the claim are not in dispute. While it is true that the amount of this claim is not in dispute, the validity of the claim remains in dispute. Consequently, Rule 408 applies and precludes admission.

74. Issue: Compromise negotiations

The correct answer is **D**. The statement that "we want to put all of this behind us" indicates that this is an attempt to compromise or settle Sam's claim. Also relevant to this determination is the fact that the meeting occurred after Sam filed his suit. Consequently, because Rule 408 excludes all statements made during settlement negotiations, the entirety of the statement is excluded. Answer A is incorrect because it assumes that the governing rule is 409 rather than 408. If this was not part of a settlement negotiation, then the only evidence excluded under Rule 409 would be the sentence about medical expenses; however, this is a case governed by Rule 408 and not Rule 409. Answer B is incorrect because the fact that the statement refers to psychiatric expenses is irrelevant. If Rule 409 applied, this would fit within the excluded type of offer of payment of medical and related expenses. Answer C is incorrect because this is not hearsay; it is a representative admission. It is a statement made by an employee about a matter within the scope of her employment that is being offered against the employer, and so it is an admission and not hearsay under Rule 801(d)(2)(D).

75. Issue: Evidence of insurance

The correct answer is **C**. Rule 411 precludes admission of evidence of insurance only if it goes to the issue of culpability. Clearly, in this case, the evidence of the name of the witness's insurer is only being asked to determine if it is the same as that of the company so that the opponent can suggest that the witness's testimony might be biased. The argument is that if the company loses and its insurer has to pay, the insurer might take it out on the witness by raising the witness' insurance premiums. This evidence does not and cannot go to the culpability of the employee witness because she is not a party. The company is a party, but the evidence of its having insurance is not being offered to show that it was negligent. Answer A is incorrect because the evidence, while not relevant to the merits, is relevant for impeachment purposes. Answer B is incorrect because the evidence is not offered to prove culpability. This evidence does not and cannot go to the culpability of the employee witness because she is not a party. The company is a party, but the evidence of its having insurance is not being offered to show that it was negligent. Answer D is incorrect because the evidence would not be admissible to establish the company's negligence.

76. Issue: Statements during plea negotiations

The correct answer is **B**. Under Rule 410, statements made during plea negotiations that result in a plea that was never withdrawn are not excluded. Here, the judge entered the plea and so the evidence is admissible. Answer A is incorrect because the statement is not hearsay; it is an admission (statement by a party offered against that party) under 801(d)(2)(A). Answer C is wrong because statements during plea negotiations are excluded only if no plea was entered or the plea was withdrawn. Here, a plea was entered and was not withdrawn. Answer D is incorrect because this was not former testimony because the statement to the prosecutor was not made under oath.

77. Issue: Witness impeachment through character evidence

The correct answer is **D**. Lois's statement is an attempt to offer opinion evidence of the defendant/witness' character for truthfulness. Under Rule 608(a)(2), the truthful character of a witness, albeit provable through reputation or opinion testimony, can only be offered after the character of that witness for untruthfulness has been impeached. Because the prosecution did not attempt to impeach the truth telling character of the defendant as a witness, the defendant cannot attempt to rehabilitate his truth-telling character. Answer A is incorrect because even though a defendant can offer reputation or opinion evidence of his good character for the purpose of proving that he acted in conformity with that character, that evidence comes in only for the purpose of proving that the defendant did not commit the crime charged. Here, the evidence of truthful character is being offered to rehabilitate Leon as a witness and not to prove that he did not commit the murder. Hence, it is Rule 608, and not Rule 404, which governs. Answer B is incorrect because under Rule 608(a)(2), the truthful character of a witness, albeit provable through reputation or opinion testimony, can only be offered after the character of that witness for untruthfulness has been impeached. Because the prosecution did not attempt to impeach the truth-telling character of the defendant as a witness, the defendant cannot attempt to rehabilitate his truth telling character. Answer C is incorrect because Rule 404 is inapplicable here, as this character evidence is being offered to rehabilitate the character of a witness and not to demonstrate the defendant's character for the purpose of showing that he did not commit the murder.

78. Issue: Witness impeachment through character evidence

The correct answer is **C**. The prosecution is offering specific acts evidence to impeach the credibility of the witness Leon by offering evidence of his character for untruthfulness. Under Rule 608(a), although the prosecution can impeach the witness, even when he is also the defendant, by attacking his character for truthfulness, this can only be accomplished on direct examination of another character witness through opinion or reputation testimony. Rule 608(b) precludes the use of specific acts evidence except during cross-examination of the primary (target) witness or of the character witness. This evidence was offered on direct examination of a character witness and therefore is an impermissible form of character testimony. Answer A is incorrect because the fact that Leon was the defendant is irrelevant to Rule 608 and Rule 404 is inapplicable to this problem because the character evidence relating to Leon's truthfulness is being used solely to impeach the credibility of him as a witness. Answer B is incorrect because this specific acts evidence is not permitted to be used to impeach the credibility of a witness under Rule 608(b). Answer D is incorrect because answer C is correct.

79. Issue: Witness impeachment through extrinsic evidence

The correct answer is **D**. Here, the prosecution is impeaching the credibility of witness Leon by offering extrinsic evidence of a prior conviction for perjury, a crime that involves false statement. Consequently, the general rule in Rule 608 — that specific instances of the witness's conduct introduced for the purpose of impeaching his character for truthfulness cannot be proved by extrinsic evidence — does not apply to convictions to the extent permitted under Rule 609. Rule 609(a)(2) sets forth a blanket rule mandating the admission of any offer of a criminal conviction of a crime involving false statement, of which perjury is a prime example. Moreover, unlike the felony convictions made admissible under the balancing test of Rule 609(a)(1), the crimes listed in Rule 609(a)(2) are not subject to the greater-than-one-year punishment standard. Hence, the fact that perjury is punishable by less than one year is irrelevant. Answer A is incorrect because the punishment standard is irrelevant for conviction of crimes involving false statement under Rule 609(a)(2). It only applies to other felony convictions under Rule 609(a)(1). Perjury is a crime involving false statement, and this problem is governed by Rule 609(a)(2) and not (a)(1). Answer B is incorrect because it assumes that this problem is governed by the balancing test of Rule 609(a)(1), but that test only applies to convictions for crimes that do not involve false statement. Perjury is a crime falling within the terms of Rule 609(a)(2), which does not impose a balancing test. Convictions of these crimes, if tendered, must be admitted. Answer C is incorrect because the Rule 608(b) provision precluding the use of extrinsic evidence to attack a witness's character for truthfulness does not apply to the introduction of criminal convictions for impeachment purposes.

80. Issue: Witness impeachment through extrinsic evidence

The correct answer is **B**. The defendant testified and therefore is impeachable under Rule 608. However, the prosecution is attempting to elicit information about specific prior acts of the defendant. Although these specific acts can be inquired into under Rule 608(b) on cross-examination of the witness whose credibility is sought to be impeached, the prosecution sought to obtain this information not through cross-examination of witness Leon, but through extrinsic evidence, i.e., through cross-examination of another witness, Lois. Although Rule 608(b) also allows specific acts by witness Leon to be inquired into on cross-examination of a character witness who testifies to Leon's truthful character through opinion or reputation testimony, Lois was not a character witness. She only offered alibi testimony, not opinion or reputation testimony of Leon's character for truthfulness. Consequently, this is specific acts evidence of character that is not admissible for impeachment purposes. Moreover, even if Lois had testified to Leon's character for truthfulness, this cross-examination asked about participating in bank robberies, which would not constitute evidence of specific acts going to the witness Leon's character for truthfulness. This extrinsic evidence is not subject to admission under Rule 609 because this is not evidence of a criminal conviction. Answer A is incorrect because Lois is not a character witness who, on cross-examination, is being asked about relevant specific acts by the person whose character for truthfulness she has testified. She only offered an alibi, not opinion or reputation testimony about Leon's character for truthfulness. Consequently, neither Rule 405(b) nor Rule 608(b)(2) is relevant here. Answer C is incorrect because the fact that Leon was a witness only means that his character for truthfulness can be attacked under Rule 608. Rule 608(b) excludes extrinsic evidence of non-convictions to challenge the truthful character of a witness. The question asked to Lois solicited extrinsic evidence of witness Leon's character. Answer D is incorrect because Lois was not asked about convictions, only about whether or not she knew that Leon had participated in armed robberies.

81. Issue: Witness impeachment through prior statement

The correct answer is **C**. Fred is a witness and his credibility can be impeached by the introduction of a prior out-of-court statement that is inconsistent with his trial testimony. As the prior statement to Bill was not made under oath, however, it is hearsay because it does not fulfill all the requirements of a non-hearsay prior inconsistent statement by a witness under Rule 801(d)(1)(A). As hearsay, it cannot be introduced for the truth of the statement that Leon killed the bartender, but it can be used for the non-hearsay purpose of impeaching the witness Fred's credibility. The only Federal Rule governing the use of prior inconsistent statements for impeachment purposes is Rule 613, and this goes only to the matter of giving the hearsay declarant a chance to explain or deny, which is assumed in the answer. Under the common law, impeachment through a prior inconsistent can be established through extrinsic evidence, as was done in this problem, because the prosecutor offered this statement not through Fred, but through Bill. Answer A is incorrect because although the prior inconsistent is hearsay because it was not made under oath in order to qualify as non-hearsay under Rule 801(d)(1)(A), it is being used for a non-hearsay purpose, i.e., to impeach the declarant/witness Fred. Therefore, it is not precluded by the hearsay rules. Answer B is incorrect because under the common law, which the federal courts look to in the absence of any express statement on this issue in the Federal Rules, prior inconsistent statements offered to impeach the credibility of a witness can be established through extrinsic evidence, as long as, per Rule 613, the declarant is given a chance at some point to explain or deny the prior out-of-court statement inconsistent with that witness's trial testimony. Answer "D" is incorrect because this would be a hearsay use of the statement, i.e., to prove the truth of the matter asserted, and this prior out-of-court statement therefore would be hearsay and not non-hearsay under Rule 801(d)(1)(A) because it was not made under oath and subject to perjury prosecution.

82. Issue: Prior inconsistent statement

The correct answer is **A**. This is a prior inconsistent statement that falls within the terms of Rule 801(d)(1)(A) because it was a witness's prior out-of-court statement made under oath, subject to perjury, and inconsistent with her trial testimony. Consequently, it is deemed not hearsay and admissible to prove the truth of the matter asserted, i.e., that Leon killed the bartender. Answer B is incorrect because Lois's grand jury testimony constitutes a prior inconsistent statement that falls within the terms of Rule 801(d)(1)(A) because it was a witness's prior out-of-court statement made under oath, subject to perjury, and inconsistent with her trial testimony. Consequently, it is deemed not hearsay and admissible to prove the truth of the matter asserted, i.e., that Leon killed the bartender. Answer C is incorrect because the statement is admissible to impeach her credibility as long as she is given an opportunity to explain or deny making it. Answer D is incorrect because answer A is correct.

83. Issue: *Morlang* rule

The correct answer is **D**. Here, the prosecution is attempting to impeach the testimony of its own witness. Rule 607 permits a party to impeach the credibility of its own witness. The problem here is that in the second trial, the prosecution cannot be considered to have been surprised by the disappointing testimony of its witness, Lois. Under the *Morlang* rule, when the prosecution tries to impeach its own witness evidence of that witness's prior inconsistent statement that otherwise would be hearsay and thus inadmissible to prove the truth of the matter asserted, the court should not permit the government to admit evidence for impeachment purposes that it could not offer for substantive purposes. Here, the witness Lois's prior inconsistent was not made under oath and therefore does not fall under Rule 801(d)(1)(A) and is hearsay. It is not admissible to establish Leon's guilt. Although it otherwise would be admissible to impeach Lois's credibility as a witness, the danger of prejudice to Leon that it would be used to assess his guilt, coupled with the fact that the prosecution knew that Lois would be an unhelpful witness, under the *Morlang* rule, is sufficient to bar its admission for all purposes. Answer A is incorrect because a party is permitted under Rule 607 to impeach its own witness. Answer B is incorrect because this is a hearsay statement as it was not made under oath and does not qualify as non-hearsay under Rule 608(d)(1)(A). Answer C is incorrect because under the *Morlang* rule, the prejudice to the defendant of this hearsay statement being used by the jury on the question of his guilt overwhelms the probative value for impeachment where the government knew in advance that its witness would not be helpful. Consequently, it had little need to impeach her because it should not have called her in the first place. So if it chooses to call her, it cannot impeach her with hearsay testimony whose contents inculpate the defendant.

84. Issue: Rehabilitation of witness

The correct answer is **C**. The defense is trying to rehabilitate the witness on the grounds of lack of bias. But under the common law (the Federal Rules do not expressly address this question), a witness cannot be rehabilitated on the matter of lack of bias unless and until that witness has been impeached on grounds of bias. The cross-examination did not attack Lois on grounds of bias. Therefore, she cannot be rehabilitated. Answer A is wrong because this fact is totally irrelevant to the question of whether a witness can be rehabilitated. Answer B is incorrect because Lois is not being impeached by this question, she is being rehabilitated, or at least the defense counsel is attempting to do so. Answer D is incorrect because although evidence of bias or lack of bias can be introduced through extrinsic evidence, it does not have to be established through extrinsic evidence.

85. Issue: Rehabilitation of witness

The correct answer is **A**. Lois is a witness and so her character for truthfulness can be attacked through opinion or reputation evidence per Rule 608. But, under Rule 608(a), her credibility cannot be supported (rehabilitated) in the form of opinion of her character for truthfulness unless and until her truthful character has been attacked. Because the cross-examination did not constitute an attack on her character for untruthfulness, she cannot be rehabilitated by offering this evidence of her truthful character. Answer B is incorrect because although this is opinion evidence, it is inadmissible because a witness's credibility cannot be rehabilitated through character evidence of truthfulness until it has first been attacked. Answer C is incorrect because even though Lois is not the defendant, a witness can be both impeached and subsequently rehabilitated through character evidence going to truthfulness. The problem here is that the witness was attempted to be rehabilitated before she had been impeached. Answer D is incorrect because the fact that this is not excluded by the hearsay rule does not mean the statement is not excluded as improper rehabilitation testimony under Rule 608(a).

86. Issue: Witness impeachment through extrinsic evidence

The correct answer is **B**. Under Rule 608(b) specific instances of the conduct of a witness for the purpose of attacking that witness's character for truthfulness, other than for a felony conviction covered by Rule 609, cannot be proved by extrinsic evidence, unless it is offered through cross-examination of the witness whose conduct is being introduced or on cross-examination of a character witness who is testifying to the character of the witness whose acts are being introduced into evidence. Here, the prosecutor offered extrinsic evidence of the witness's prior acts going to untruthfulness on direct (not cross) examination of a witness who is being called to impeach the credibility of the prior witness, Lois, and that is prohibited by Rule 608(b). Answer A is incorrect because although the prosecutor can attack the credibility of the witness, it cannot do it with extrinsic evidence of a non-conviction unless it is offered through cross-examination of the witness whose conduct is being introduced or on cross-examination of a character witness who is testifying to the character of the witness whose acts are being introduced into evidence. This extrinsic evidence was not offered through such a cross-examination, and so it is inadmissible under Rule 608(b). Answer C is incorrect because even though the witness denied making the statement, as Rule 608(b) precludes the introduction of extrinsic evidence of the witness's prior acts going to truthfulness, the prosecutor is stuck with the witness's answer and cannot contradict it with extrinsic evidence of a non-conviction. All the prosecutor can do is to try to get the witness to admit to the prior acts. Answer D is incorrect because answer B is correct.

87. Issue: Witness impeachment for bias

The correct answer is **C**. Charles was a witness and can be impeached on grounds of bias. Moreover, under the common law (the Federal Rules do not cover the subject of impeachment on the grounds of bias), bias can be established through extrinsic evidence. Here, the prosecution is offering extrinsic evidence, through the testimony of Frank, going to the witness Charles' bias. This is permitted. Answer A is incorrect because although character for truthfulness cannot be established through extrinsic evidence, this is evidence going to bias, not to character for truthfulness. Answer B is incorrect because a witness's bias can be established through extrinsic evidence. Answer D is incorrect because the evidence is relevant to the question of the witness's credibility.

88. Issue: Witness impeachment for incapacity

The correct answer is **D**. Charles was a witness and can be impeached on grounds of incapacity. The question here is whether or not evidence of being under psychiatric treatment at the time of the event or the time of his testimony is probative of the witness's lack of capacity to testify accurately.

Presumably, being treated for fear of heights does not have any impact on the witness's ability to remember, perceive, or express himself concerning the events in question. Consequently, this evidence is not evidence of incapacity or any other form of impeachment and is irrelevant to any issue on the merits of the case. Answer A is incorrect because this is not admissible impeachment testimony as it is not probative of his lack of capacity. Answer B is incorrect because this is not hearsay testimony. Answer C is incorrect because extrinsic evidence can be used to establish bias or incapacity of a witness.

89. Issue: Witness impeachment for bias

The correct answer is **B**. Peggy is a witness and her testimony can be impeached on the ground of bias. The testimony from Charles is extrinsic evidence. If it is being used to contradict Peggy's testimony on a matter unrelated to either the merits of the case or the witness Peggy's bias or incapacity, it would be excluded under the collateral evidence rule. This evidence not only contradicts Peggy's testimony that they had been going out on a first date, but it is relevant to establishing her bias in favor of the defendant. Consequently, it is admissible extrinsic evidence of the witness Peggy's bias and not excluded under the collateral evidence rule. Answer A is incorrect because this evidence not only contradicts Peggy's testimony that they had been going out on a first date, but it is relevant to establishing her bias in favor of the defendant. Consequently, it is admissible extrinsic evidence of the witness Peggy's bias and not excluded under the collateral evidence rule. Answer C is incorrect because extrinsic evidence can be used to establish a witness's bias and that is the purpose of this extrinsic evidence, which not only contradicts the witness's testimony but is evidence of her bias in favor of the defendant. Answer D is incorrect because answer B is correct.

90. Issue: Lay opinion testimony

The correct answer is **B**. This is clearly opinion evidence by a police officer. But although Rule 701 permits lay opinion testimony, it must be based on the witness's first-hand knowledge. The police officer's testimony is predicated on information concerning Leon's hatred for the whiskey industry that he heard from someone else. He did not get this information first hand from observing Leon. Consequently, it is inadmissible lay opinion testimony. It cannot come in under Rule 702 as expert testimony because even if this opinion calls for the possession of specialized (psychiatric) knowledge (which it probably does not), the officer has not been qualified as an psychiatric expert. Answer A is incorrect because although Rule 701 permits lay opinion testimony, it must be based on the witness's first-hand knowledge. The police officer's testimony is predicated on information concerning Leon's hatred for the whiskey industry that he heard from someone else. He did not get this information first hand from observing Leon. Consequently, it is inadmissible lay opinion testimony. Answer C is incorrect because the officer's experience is not relevant to meeting the requirements for lay testimony in Rule 701. Moreover, the evidence cannot be admitted under Rule 702 as expert testimony because this testimony does not call for specialized police training skills and the officer has not been qualified as a psychiatric expert. Answer D is wrong because the testimony is not hearsay, as the witness is not repeating what he heard outside of the courtroom about Leon. He is merely giving his opinion as to the motive for killing the bartender.

91. Issue: Attorney-client privilege

The correct answer is **C**. Because the defendant has asserted an insanity plea, the prosecution is seeking to compel attorney Paula to testify as to her client's demeanor during the conversation to establish that he was not insane at the time of the murder. Consequently, the prosecution is not asking the attorney to reveal a "communication" by the client and therefore the information is not privileged. Answer A is incorrect because this would not be hearsay; it is an admission by a defendant. Answer B is incorrect because as the defendant has asserted an insanity plea, the prosecution is seeking to compel attorney Paula to testify as to her client's demeanor during the conversation to establish that he was not insane at the time of the murder. Consequently, the prosecution is not asking the attorney to reveal a statement or "communication" by the client and therefore the information is not privileged. Answer D is incorrect because the fact that this is an admission is irrelevant to the question of whether it is a confidential communication covered by the attorney-client privilege.

92. Issue: Attorney-client privilege

The correct answer is **D**. The presence of the cellmate in the cell at the time of the conversation broke the confidentiality of the conversation and, therefore, the communications are not privileged and the attorney can be forced to disclose the contents. Answer A is wrong because the presence of the cellmate in the cell at the time of the conversation broke the confidentiality of the conversation and, therefore, the communications are not privileged and the attorney can be forced to disclose the contents. Answer B is incorrect because the issue here is not whether there was an attorney-client relationship, but whether the communication was made confidentially. Answer C is incorrect because the issue here is not whether there was an attorney-client relationship, but whether the communication was made confidentially.

93. Issue: Attorney-client privilege

The correct answer is **B**. The issue here is whether Steve is an agent of the attorney Paula and therefore covered by the privilege. Because Steve was employed after the creation of the attorney-client relationship and was working to assist the attorney in the presentation of a legal defense, Steve is covered by the privilege. Answer A is incorrect because as Steve was employed after the creation of the attorney-client relationship and was working to assist the attorney in the presentation of a legal defense, Steve is covered by the privilege. Answer C is incorrect because whether or not the statement is admissible as an admission and not hearsay is irrelevant to the question of whether the material is covered by the attorney–client privilege. Answer D is incorrect because answer B is correct.

94. Issue: Attorney-client privilege

The correct answer is **D**. The statement was made in confidence during the life of the attorney-client privilege. It is therefore privileged unless the client waived the privilege. However, actions by the attorney that are acquiesced to or encouraged by the client are deemed an implied waiver by the client. Here, the client participated in revealing that part of the conversation that related to six of the seven burglaries. The question is whether under the fairness doctrine this constitutes a waiver of the privilege for the undisclosed part of that conversation. When part of a confidential conversation is revealed in a judicial proceeding, the courts apply the fairness doctrine to compel the disclosure of the rest of that particular conversation. But where, as here, the disclosure is made in an extrajudicial setting, the courts tend not to apply the fairness doctrine and tend to hold that the client has not waived privilege as to the entire contents of the conversation. Consequently, this statement is privileged and the client will not be deemed to have waived the privilege by participating in a public disclosure of part of the conversation. Answer A is wrong because the confidential communication occurred during the life of the attorney-client privilege. Consequently, the privilege, if it has not been waived, will apply after the termination of that attorney-client relationship. So, the fact that the attorney–client relationship did not exist at the time of the attempt to compel the disclosure does not figure in the answer to this question. Answer B is incorrect because the privilege is held by the client and, therefore, can be waived only by the client, not by the attorney. Actions by the attorney that are acquiesced to or encouraged by the client can result in an implied waiver by the client, however. Here, the client participated in revealing that part of the conversation that related to six of the seven burglaries. The question is whether under the fairness doctrine this constitutes a waiver of the privilege for the undisclosed part of that conversation. When part of a confidential conversation is revealed in a judicial proceeding, the courts apply the fairness doctrine to compel the disclosure of the rest of that particular conversation. But where, as here, the disclosure is made in an extrajudicial setting, the courts tend not to apply the fairness doctrine and tend not find that the client has waived privilege as to the entire contents of the conversation. Answer C is incorrect because it is the party asserting the privilege, not the party opposing the privilege, who shoulders the burden of proving that the privilege should be applied.

95. Issue: Adverse spousal testimony privilege

The correct answer is **C**. Marge can testify because the privilege against adverse spousal testimony is held only by the testifying spouse. The non-testifying spouse no longer can preclude the other spouse from testifying adversely to his interests. Because Marge is willing to testify, she can testify. However, the spousal privilege covering confidential communications made during the life of the marriage exists and operates to preclude the wife from revealing the contents of a confidential communication made during the marriage. Even though the pair was separated when the conversation took place, the common law privilege requires only that the parties to the conversation be married at the time of the communication; they need not be in love or even living together. Thus, the privilege applies with respect to his statement to Marge about his role in the murder. Answer A is incorrect because the historic privilege held by each spouse allowing each one to prevent the other from testifying adversely to their interest was significantly curtailed by the Supreme Court in *Trammel v. U.S.* There, the Court interpreted Rule 501 to permit the federal to modify the extant rule as dictated by reason and experience, and it held that the privilege no longer was held by the non-testifying spouse. It is now held only by the testifying spouse. So, if a spouse wants to testify, she can and the husband cannot stop her from taking the stand. That does not mean that Marge can reveal confidential communications from the husband made during the life of the marriage, but answer A states that the wife will not be permitted to testify at all. That is incorrect. Answer B is incorrect because the question is whether or not Marge can testify at all, not whether the particular out-of-court statement made by her husband during the phone conversation is admissible. That statement is an admission under Rule 801(d)(2)(A) and is, therefore, not hearsay. That fact is irrelevant to this question, however. Answer D is incorrect because answer C is correct.

96. Issue: Spousal privilege for confidential communications

The correct answer is **B**. The statement was made during the life of the marriage. However, among the recognized exceptions to the spousal privilege is the case in which one spouse is prosecuted for a crime against the other spouse or any of their children. Because this is a criminal prosecution of the husband for the attempted murder of the wife, the exception applies and the statement will not be privileged. Answer A is incorrect because although the statement was made during the life of the marriage, among the recognized exceptions to the spousal privilege is the case in which one spouse is prosecuted for a crime against the other spouse or any of their children. Because this is a criminal prosecution of the husband for the attempted murder of the wife, the exception applies and the statement will not be privileged. Answer C is incorrect because even though the out-of-court statement was made by the defendant and is being used against the defendant and, therefore, constitutes an admission and not hearsay under Rule 801(d)(2)(A), the fact that the statement is not hearsay does not mean it must be admitted. It would not have been admitted if the privilege had applied. A reason the statement is admissible is because it is not privileged. Thus, it being an admission is not the sole reason that it is admissible. Answer D is incorrect because answer B is correct.

97. Issue: Crime-fraud exception to spousal privilege

The correct answer is **C**. This communication was made during the life of the marriage. However, among the recognized exceptions to the spousal privilege is the crime-fraud exception, which does not extend the privilege to confidential communications concerning the planned commission of a future crime or fraud. This statement by William is a statement concerning a future crime, and so falls within the crime-fraud exception to the spousal privilege. Because William is not being charged with attempted murder of his wife, the exception to the spousal privilege for otherwise privileged statements used in prosecutions of one spouse for a crime against the other spouse does not apply. Answer A is incorrect because although this communication was made during the life of the marriage, among the recognized exceptions to the spousal privilege is the crime-fraud exception, which does not extend the privilege to confidential communications concerning the planned commission of a future crime or fraud. This statement by William is a statement concerning a future crime, and so falls within the crime-fraud exception to the spousal privilege. Answer B is incorrect because the fact that William is being prosecuted for the attempted murder of the boyfriend and not of his wife only means that the exception to the spousal privilege for otherwise privileged statements used in prosecutions of one spouse for a crime against the other spouse does not apply. Answer D is incorrect because the fact that the statement refers to a crime he will commit against someone else is irrelevant to the application of the crime-fraud exception to the spousal privilege. Any statement made by a spouse that relates to the commission of any future crime is not privileged.

98. Issue: Authentication

The correct answer is **B**. Under Rule 901, the threshold for determining authenticity for purposes of resolving questions of admissibility is low. All the proponent of the evidence has to produce is sufficient evidence, circumstantial or otherwise, that would allow a reasonable jury to conclude that the evidence is what it purports to be. Gaps in the chain of custody do not go to admissibility. This is a factor that the jury can consider in determining how much weight to assign to this evidence. Answer A is incorrect because Under Rule 901, the threshold for determining authenticity for purposes of resolving questions of admissibility is low. All the proponent of the evidence has to produce is sufficient evidence, circumstantial or otherwise, that would allow a reasonable jury to conclude that the evidence is what it purports to be. Gaps in the chain of custody do not go to admissibility. This is a factor that the jury can consider in determining how much weight to assign to this evidence. Answer C is incorrect because the fact that this gun has blood on it does not establish that it is authentic, i.e., that it was the gun taken from the murder scene. Had the blood been determined to be that of the decedent, that might be a different matter, but the problem does not include that fact. Answer D is incorrect because answer B is correct.

99. Issue: Chain of custody

The correct answer is **D**. The prosecution is not seeking to introduce the gun into evidence. Consequently, its authenticity is not in issue here; however, the relevance (probativity) of Laura's testimony turns on whether the gun she tested is actually the gun that was picked up at the alleged crime scene. So, the chain of custody is relevant to determining the relevance of her testimony. Trial judges have broad discretion under Rule 401 in determining relevance, and the courts hold that gaps in the chain of custody are relevant not to admissibility of this sort of testimony, but to the weight that is assigned it by the jury. Answer A is incorrect because the prosecution is not seeking to introduce the gun into evidence, thus its authenticity is not in issue here. Answer B is incorrect because although the chain of custody is relevant to the issue of the relevance of this expert testimony, trial judges have broad discretion under Rule 401 in determining relevance and the courts hold that gaps in the chain of custody are relevant not to admissibility of this sort of testimony, but to the weight that is assigned it by the jury. Answer C is incorrect because the expert would be testifying as to her observations and not as to any out-of-court statement, so her testimony would not be hearsay.

100. Issue: Best evidence rule

The correct answer is **C**. Because the witness is testifying as to her observations and conclusions and not as to the contents of her report, the best evidence rule does not apply. Laura is offering expert opinion testimony, which will be admitted under Rule 702 as long as she is qualified as a witness. Answer A is incorrect because as the witness is testifying as to her observations and conclusions and not as to the contents of her report, the best evidence rule does not apply. The fact that the information that she is testifying to is also contained in a writing does not invoke the best evidence rule when the testimony does not refer to that writing. Answer B is incorrect because Laura is not repeating the contents of that out-of-court document nor is the document being offered into evidence. Even if it were, however, the hearsay exception for business records or public records clearly would apply. Answer D is incorrect because answer C is correct.

101. Issue: Relevance

The correct answer is **C**. This real evidence meets the Rule 401 definition of relevance because it is probative of a material proposition in the case — that the victim actually died as well as the cause of death. Under Rule 403, however, the trial judge has the discretion to exclude evidence whose prejudicial impact substantially outweighs its probative value. This sort of highly inflammatory evidence is typically the kind of evidence whose probative value is substantially outweighed by the emotional impact it will have on the jury. This is a balancing test. Answer A is incorrect because under the balancing test of Rule 403, otherwise relevant evidence can be excluded because of its prejudicial impact. Relevance is not always a sufficient basis for admissibility. Answer B is wrong because this evidence meets the relevancy standards of probativity and materiality. Answer D is wrong because answer C is correct.

102. Issue: Relevance

The correct answer is **D**. Rule 404(a)(1) allows the defendant to offer evidence of a relevant trait of his or her character through opinion or reputation evidence, and all four of these witnesses are testifying as to a relevant (nonviolent) character trait of the defendant. The fourth witness's testimony meets the requirements of Rule 404(a)(1). Under Rule 403, however, a trial judge has the discretion to exclude otherwise relevant information if it is deemed to be cumulative, i.e., will cause undue delay and waste time. Here, although the evidence offered by the fourth character witness is both relevant and admissible under Rule 404(a)(1), it is cumulative and would be excluded under Rule 403. Answer A is wrong because the fact that it is admissible character evidence is not dispositive. It still can be excluded under the balancing test of Rule 403 if deemed cumulative and a waste of time and cause of undue delay, and that would be the case here. Answer B is incorrect because this is otherwise admissible character evidence under Rule 404(a)(1) because it was offered by the defendant and is reputation testimony relating to a pertinent (nonviolent) trait of character of the defendant. Answer C is wrong because reputation evidence falls within the Rule 803(19) exception to the hearsay rule.

103. Issue: Character evidence in a civil case

The correct answer is **B**. The evidence of prior acts of speeding is being used to prove that the defendant is a speeder, and this makes it more likely (probative) of the fact that he was speeding when the accident occurred. This is an attempt to make circumstantial use of character evidence to prove action in conformity with that character trait. Rule 404(a) prohibits character evidence to prove conformity in all civil cases except where it is being used to prove the character of a witness. Joe was not a witness as the evidence was offered in the plaintiff's case-in-chief. Although he is the defendant, the exception in Rule 404(a)(1) permitting the introduction of evidence of a defendant's character applies only in criminal cases. Thus, this evidence of the character of a non-witness in a civil case is inadmissible. Answer A is incorrect because the fact that the plaintiff is offering this evidence is not dispositive. If this had been a criminal case, under Rule 404(a)(1), the prosecution could not offer evidence of the defendant's character until the defendant had opened the door. This is a civil case, however, and Rule 404 permits character evidence in a civil case only when it goes to the character of a witness. Answer C is wrong because the fact that Joe is not a witness is one of the reasons for excluding the evidence, not for admitting it. Answer D is wrong because answer B is correct.

104. Issue: Non-character use of prior acts evidence

The correct answer is **A**. The prosecution is offering evidence of the criminal defendant's past act through evidence of a prior conviction. Under Rule 404(a)(1), the prosecution cannot offer evidence of the defendant's bad character trait to show that the defendant acted in conformity with that trait unless and until the defendant has offered otherwise admissible (through reputation or opinion) evidence of a pertinent character trait. The defendant has not opened the door here, as this evidence was offered during the prosecution's case-in-chief. Moreover, even if the defendant had opened the door, which it did not, per Rule 404(b), the prosecution could only offer evidence of the defendant's character to show action in conformity therewith through opinion or reputation testimony. Here, the prosecution offered evidence of a prior conviction. These rules do not apply to the facts of this case, however, because although Rule 404(b) prohibits past acts evidence to establish character to show conformity, this rule also provides that past acts evidence is admissible if it is not being used to prove character, but something else. Here, the evidence of the prior robbery is not being offered to prove that the defendant is a thieving person (character), and so it is more likely that she committed this robbery. It is being offered to prove that the defendant had the combination to the safe, i.e., the opportunity to commit this crime. Therefore, the evidence is admissible under Rule 404(b). Answer B is incorrect because this evidence is not offered to prove the defendant's character, but to prove opportunity to commit the crime by having the combination to the safe, which helps establish opportunity to commit the alleged crime. Answer C is incorrect because this evidence is not offered to prove the defendant's character. If it was offered for this purpose, this past acts evidence would be excluded under Rule 404(a)(1) and 404(b) because the defendant did not open the door and because it comes in the form of specific acts, and not reputation or opinion, evidence. Answer D is wrong because under the balancing test of Rule 403, the prejudicial value would have to substantially outweigh, not just outweigh, the probative value. Moreover, there is no prejudicial impact associated with this evidence as that term is used in Rule 403.

105. Issue: Evidence of liability insurance

The correct answer is **A**. Under Rule 411, evidence of either insurance or the absence of insurance against liability is inadmissible when offered to prove whether the person acted negligently. Although the evidence would be admitted to prove something else, such as ownership, control, or bias, this answer merely states that it is irrelevant to prove negligence. Answer B is incorrect because Rule 411 applies to evidence of either the presence or absence of insurance. Answer C is incorrect because although evidence of insurance or lack of insurance could be offered to prove ownership or control, if, as this answer assumes, the defendant Patricia does not deny ownership or control of the car, that issue is not in dispute. Answer D is wrong because answer A is correct.

106. Issue: Evidence of compromise

The correct answer is **B**. Although it is true that Rule 408 excludes evidence of accepting a compromise when that evidence is offered to prove liability for, the invalidity or, or amount of a disputed claim, this rule does not exclude such evidence if offered to prove something else. Here, the evidence is offered to impeach the credibility of the witness uncle on the ground that he is biased in favor of the defendant Patricia. So, it is permissible to show the uncle's bias.

Answer A is wrong because the fact that this is evidence of the settlement of a disputed claim does not automatically result in exclusion under Rule 408. That rule excludes the evidence only if it is offered to prove the validity or invalidity of a disputed claim or of its amount. Here, the evidence is offered to prove bias of the witness. Answer C is wrong because this evidence is relevant to establish the bias of the witness. Answer D is wrong because answer B is correct.

107. Issue: Evidence of compromise

The correct answer is **B**. Rule 408 excludes more than evidence of a compromise offer or the acceptance of a compromise offer. It also excludes statements made during the course of compromise negotiations that relate to the claim. There is a minor exception applicable to criminal cases, but this is a civil case, so the exception is inapplicable. This statement by the defendant goes directly to the issue of negligence, and as a statement made during settlement negotiations, it is excluded. Answer A is wrong because this is an admission, as it is a statement by a party that is being offered against the party. Thus, it is deemed not to be hearsay under Rule 801(d)(2)(A). Answer C is incorrect because statements made during settlement negotiations, as well as the fact of the offer or acceptance of a compromise offer, are covered by the Rule 408 exclusion. Answer D is incorrect because this is a party admission and, therefore, not hearsay in the first place.

108. Issue: Evidence of compromise

The correct answer is **D**. Rule 408 only excludes evidence of statements offering to compromise a claim that is disputed as to its validity or amount. Patricia made this offer the day after the accident, months before suit had been filed. Consequently, there was no disputed claim in existence at the time she made these remarks. Consequently, the statements are not covered by the Rule 408 exclusion. Answer A is wrong because this is not evidence of a compromise offer of a disputed claim. Answer B is wrong because although the witness is recounting the content of an out-of-court statement to prove the truth of that statement (that Patricia was drunk when she crashed her car into the plaintiff's home), the statement was made by a party and is being offered against that party. Hence, it is an admission and therefore it is deemed not to be hearsay under Rule 801(d)(2)(A). Answer C is wrong because this is an admission and therefore not hearsay in the first place, and so there is no need to search for an exception to the hearsay doctrine.

109. Issue: Character evidence in a civil suit

The correct answer is **A**. This evidence of falling asleep on the job is being offered as circumstantial evidence that Patricia acted consistently with that behavior and fell asleep when she was driving. Character evidence to establish action in conformity with that character is inadmissible in civil cases except when, per Rule 404(a)(3), it is offered to impeach the character of a witness. Patricia was not a witness, however, and so this evidence is excluded under Rule 404(a). Even if this had been a criminal case, which it is not, the evidence of character would be inadmissible because it does not come in the form of opinion or reputation evidence but, instead, is evidence of past acts. Thus, such past acts evidence in a criminal case would be precluded by Rule 405(a). Answer B is incorrect because although evidence of habit is admissible to show action consistently with that habit in a civil case, this is not evidence of habit within the meaning of Rule 406. That rule requires the conduct to be a regular response to a commonly repeated event or set of events, and this evidence of a one example of sleeping on the job does not meet that standard. Answer C is wrong because the fact that Patricia put her good character into issue does not permit the plaintiff to offer character evidence in a civil case against the defendant when the defendant never took the stand to testify. Answer D is wrong because Mary is testifying as to what she saw and not as to the contents of an out-of-court statement.

110. Issue: Non-character use of past acts evidence
The correct answer is **B**. Rules 404(a)(1) and 405(a) combine to tell us that the prosecution cannot offer evidence of the defendant's pertinent trait of character to prove action in conformity with that character trait unless and until the defendant has opened the door by offering evidence of his good character, and that even then, the evidence must come in the form of opinion and reputation and not, as here, evidence of past acts. It is true that the defendant has not opened the door and this is past acts evidence; however, under Rule 405(b), these rules do not apply if the evidence is offered not to prove character to show action in conformity therewith, but rather, to prove something else such as preparation or a common plan. Here, evidence of his prior shootings of other high school teachers is admissible for the limited purpose of proving that he had a common plan of shooting his high school teachers, although not for the purpose of establishing that having shot other teachers, it is likely that he shot this one. Answer A is incorrect because the fact that the prosecution offered this evidence before the defendant opened the door is inapplicable since the evidence is offered to prove the defendant's common plan and not that he has a criminal predisposition and acted in conformity with that trait in this case. Answer C is incorrect because these two events do not meet the Rule 406 definition of habit in that it does not demonstrate a regular response to a commonly repeated event or set of events. Answer D is incorrect because the fact that the defendant did not open the door is not relevant here, as the evidence is being offered to prove something other than action in conformity with a general criminal predisposition.

111. Issue: Authentication of real evidence
The correct answer is **B**. The bag of powder is real evidence, and therefore must be authenticated to establish that this bag is, in fact, the bag taken from the defendant's home. Authentication could be established under Rule 901 in either of two ways; because of the distinctive characteristics of this particular piece of evidence, or through establishing a chain of custody. Neither has been accomplished here. There is no indication in the facts that the white powder

taken from the house had any particularly distinctive characteristics that are present in the bag offered up by the prosecution. Nor has the prosecution established a sufficient chain of custody, because there is no evidence about the custody of this bag from the time the officer brought it to the lab until its presentation at trial. Without such authentication, the evidence is inadmissible. Answer A is wrong because not all real evidence is automatically admissible; it must be authenticated and it was not authenticated here. Answer C is wrong because this fact is irrelevant to the admissibility of the bag. Answer D is wrong because the fact that evidence is highly probative does not guarantee its admissibility. Real evidence needs to be authenticated, and this piece of real evidence was not.

112. Issue: Best evidence rule

The correct answer is **B**. Although the best evidence rule codified at Rule 1002 requires the introduction of the original or duplicate of a writing, the rule only applies when the evidence is being offered of the contents of a writing. The fact that a witness testifies to facts that also happen to be contained in a writing does not invoke the best evidence rule when the witness does not refer in his testimony to that writing. Here, the witness did not refer to the writing, so the best evidence rule is inapplicable. He offered an expert opinion, but was qualified to do so and testified from his personal knowledge. Answer A is wrong because the best evidence rule does not apply here as the witness did not testify to the contents of a writing, but only to facts that also happen to be contained in a writing to which the witness did not refer. Answer C is wrong because real evidence was not sought to be admitted, only the opinion of the witness. Answer D is wrong because an expert can give an opinion after he or she has been qualified as an expert, which was the case here.

113. Issue: Best evidence rule

The correct answer is **D**. The best evidence rule only requires the admission of an original of a writing, recording, or photo; it does not require introduction of other forms of real evidence (the uniform) just because a piece of real evidence that is not a writing is being discussed through testimony rather than through admission of the actual piece of evidence. So, the best evidence rule is irrelevant here. Also, real evidence has to be authenticated only when it is offered into evidence. Here, a witness referred to something that would be considered real evidence (the uniform), but no uniform was presented. So, there is no need for authentication. Answer A is wrong because the Best evidence rule does not preclude extrinsic evidence concerning a piece of real evidence that does not constitute a writing, recording, or photo. Here, the witness referred to a piece of real evidence that was not a writing, recording, or photo, so the Best evidence rule is inapplicable. Answer B is wrong because no uniform was produced as evidence, so there was no real evidence that needed to be authenticated. Referring in testimony to something that is real evidence does not invoke the requirement of authentication. The witness is simply testifying as to what he saw. Answer C is wrong because this is not

evidence of the defendant's character trait offered to prove action in conformity with that trait.

114. Issue: Confrontation Clause

The correct answer is **A**. Lamar's statement before the grand jury is testimonial
in nature under the Supreme Court's ruling in *Crawford v. Washington* (2004)
because it described a past event in connection with a criminal prosecution.
Although the declarant is alive and was called as a witness, because he invoked
his constitutional rights and refused to testify, he is unavailable for cross-examination at trial about the grand jury testimony. Moreover, because there was no
opportunity for the defense to cross-examine the declarant when he testified
before the grand jury, the Sixth Amendment Confrontation Clause precludes
the introduction of this testimonial declaration. Thus, even though this hearsay
testimony of this unavailable witness would fit within the declaration against
penal interest exception to the hearsay rule, the Court in *Crawford* ruled that
the Confrontation Clause precludes the admission of otherwise admissible
hearsay statements that are deemed to be "testimonial" unless the defendant
had the opportunity to cross-examine the declarant either at trial or when the
out-of-court statement was made. There was no such opportunity here, and so
admission would be unconstitutional. Answer B is incorrect because this testimony does not fall within that exception; Rule 804(b)(1) applies only where
the party against whom it is offered had an opportunity and motive to cross-
examine the declarant. No such opportunity existed either before the grand
jury or at trial, because the declarant invoked his constitutional right to refuse
to testify. Answer C is incorrect because although this is an out-of-court
statement offered to prove the truth of its contents, it falls within the declaration against interest exception, so it is not excludable hearsay. Answer D is
wrong because although this statement does fall within the hearsay exception
for declarations against penal interest (because the declarant Lamar is unavailable by dint of refusing to testify), it is still barred from being introduced against
the criminal defendant because of the Confrontation Clause as it is testimonial
in nature and the defendant had no opportunity to cross-examine the declarant
either at trial or before the grand jury.

115. Issue: Confrontation Clause

The correct answer is **B**. Lamar's statement before the grand jury is testimonial
in nature under the Supreme Court's ruling in *Crawford v. Washington* (2004)
because it described a past event in connection with a criminal prosecution.
The declarant Lamar is dead and therefore unavailable for cross-examination at
trial about the grand jury testimony. Additionally, there was no opportunity for
the defense to cross-examine the declarant when he testified before the grand
jury. Under *Crawford*, where a "testimonial" hearsay statement otherwise
would be admissible because it falls within an exception, if the criminal
defendant against whom it is offered never had the opportunity to cross-examine the declarant when the testimonial statement was made or was repeated at
trial, the Sixth Amendment Confrontation Clause precludes the introduction

of this testimonial declaration. Thus, even though this hearsay testimony of this unavailable witness would fit within the declaration against penal interest exception to the hearsay rule, it is true that the declarant Lamar was unavailable for cross-examination when his statement was made in front of the jury and now, because he is dead, he is unavailable for cross-examination at trial. Ordinarily, under *Crawford*, this would render this testimonial statement inadmissible pursuant to the dictates of the Confrontation Clause. However, the declarant Lamar was made unavailable for trial by the act of the defendant Vernon in killing him. In *Giles v. California* (2008), the Court created an exception to the *Crawford* doctrine where the declarant was made unavailable for trial through an action taken by the defendant for the purpose of preventing the declarant from testifying at trial. This case clearly falls within the exception, and so the hearsay testimony will be admitted because it falls within the declaration against interest exception and the dead declarant is unavailable, as required by Rule 804(b)(3). Answer A is incorrect because of the *Giles* exception to the *Crawford* rule, which eliminates the Confrontation Clause as a basis for exclusion of an otherwise admissible hearsay statement when the declarant's unavailability for cross-examination was the result of an act taken by the defendant for the purpose of preventing the declarant from testifying at trial. Because that is what happened here, the evidence is not excluded by the Confrontation Clause. Answer C is incorrect because although hearsay, this statement by a now-unavailable declarant fits within the declaration against penal interest exception to hearsay found in Rule 804(b)(3). Answer D is wrong because this was an out-of-court statement by Lamar, who is not a party to this case. Admissions are statements made by or attributed to a party when offered against that party.